William George Black

What are teinds?

An account of the history of tithes in Scotland

William George Black

What are teinds?
An account of the history of tithes in Scotland

ISBN/EAN: 9783743345355

Manufactured in Europe, USA, Canada, Australia, Japa

Cover: Foto ©ninafisch / pixelio.de

Manufactured and distributed by brebook publishing software (www.brebook.com)

William George Black

What are teinds?

WHAT ARE TEINDS?

AN ACCOUNT OF

THE HISTORY OF TITHES

IN SCOTLAND

BY

WILLIAM GEORGE BLACK

AUTHOR OF 'THE PAROCHIAL ECCLESIASTICAL LAW OF SCOTLAND'

EDINBURGH
WILLIAM GREEN & SONS
LAW PUBLISHERS
1893

PREFACE

In the following chapters an attempt has been made to indicate the historical development of the law of tithes in Scotland. On this subject there has been a good deal of misunderstanding, at which no one can be surprised who has attempted to grapple with the intricacies and anomalies of parochial ecclesiastical law. By tracing the law of tithe-paying from its first civic enactment under Charlemagne, through English practice, down to the time of its introduction into Scotland by King David, an opportunity is afforded of gaining a clearer idea of the history of the matter; and so far as was possible I have avoided the use of the technical expressions with which this subject is superabundantly supplied, and which go far to make any account of Teind Court procedure unintelligible to all but practitioners in that court.

The words Teind and Tithe have the same meaning, and describe the tenth part of the annual produce of the soil cultivated by man, or of the profits of his industry, set aside for the maintenance of teachers of religion, but 'Teind' is used in Scotland more frequently than 'Tithe.'

I am indebted to Mr. Wm. C. Bishop, W.S., for courteously perusing the proofs of the summary, in Chapter V., of the present position of Teinds in Scotland. The responsibility for the book as a whole, however, is entirely upon myself.

WILLIAM GEORGE BLACK.

88 WEST REGENT STREET,
   GLASGOW, *May* 1893.

CONTENTS

CHAPTER I
PAGE
The Civil Institution of Tithes in Europe, . . 1-10

CHAPTER II
Tithes in England, 970 to 1066, ... 11-20

CHAPTER III
Tithes in Scotland before the Reformation: 1058 to 1560, 21-41

CHAPTER IV
Tithes in Scotland during the Reformation Period and subsequently: 1560 to 1628, ... 42-65

CHAPTER V
Teinds in the Present Day, ... 66-91

CHAPTER VI
The Survival of the Old Church, ... 92-110

WHAT ARE TEINDS?

AN ACCOUNT OF THE HISTORY OF TITHES IN SCOTLAND

CHAPTER I

THE CIVIL INSTITUTION OF TITHES IN EUROPE

THE theory of the legal devotion of one-tenth of the produce of man's cultivation of the soil to the maintenance of religion and of its servants owes its origin to the Jews, but for its recognition in the Christian civil law we must look to the reign of Charlemagne. There is scarcely any other subject which more effectually illustrates the rise of the Church of Rome, or which can be less understood without recourse to the pages of history, than tithes. From 476, when the Western Empire ended, and Constantinople, instead of Rome, became the nominal capital of the nominal successors of Augustus, the Church steadily became more and more a political as well as a religious power. Her progress was irregular, for the character of her Popes varied; but it never ceased. In the absence of Cæsar, the heir of St. Peter became with every century more markedly the chief man in Rome. The Church, whatever her faults, was fulfilling her mission in sending missionaries to the heathen, and in succouring the poor at home. Such demands upon the Church's purse necessitated the creation of sufficient revenues, but they were long defective. Bit by bit estates were given her, or were acquired by purchase; but the attention of the clergy was directed, not unnaturally, to the restoration of the Levitical doctrine of the religion which they taught—a restoration which would have brought into the treasury a more or less regular income from tithes. They are frequently referred to in the early history of the Church, but no trace of enforcement under even ecclesiastical penalties is found earlier than the Council of Rouen in 630. Their payment as a religious duty was certainly recognised not long after 567, the date of the second Council of Tours, and had been taught on Scriptural analogy by St. Augustine and St. Jerome, and positively by Cæsarius, Archbishop of Arles, 503-544. To enforce the collection of tithes was, however, in the nature of things impossible when there was no power other than the Pope's to see to the payment, and his authority as yet was quite inadequate to the task.

It is therefore to the time when Charlemagne rescued Rome from the fear of the Lombards, and was welcomed by Hadrian as the deliverer of both Church and people, that we have to look for the dawn of a real civil connection between the Church and the State; and accordingly it is from an ordinance made by Charlemagne as King of the Franks, in a general assembly of his Estates, spiritual and temporal, in 778-779, that any outline of the history of tithes must start. The ordinance was in the following terms:—'Concerning tithes, it is ordained that every man give his tithe, and that they be dispensed according to the bishop's commandment.'

A Capitular for Saxony in 789 appointed tithes to be paid out of all public property, and that all men, 'whether noble, or gentle, or of lower degree,' should 'give according to God's commandment, to the churches and priests, of their substance and labour: as God has given to each Christian, so ought he to repay a part to God.' A Capitular of 800 made the payment of tithes universal within the fiscal domain of the whole Frankish kingdom.[1]

From the year last mentioned dates the rise of the Church as Catholic. When on Christmas Day, 800, Leo III. placed the crown on the German king's head in the basilica of St. Peter at Rome, as he knelt before the high altar, with the words, 'Karolo Augusto a Deo coronato magno et pacifico imperatori vita et victoria,' then, as has been truly said, 'modern history begins.'

Henceforward the political and religious unity of the world was, at least in theory, an accomplished fact. The Holy Roman Church and the Holy Roman Empire were but two aspects of one idea. The spiritual aspect of the Visible Church was represented by the Pope, the political by the Emperor. It was an attractive idea which rules all mediæval history, and for a time it was not only a metaphysical conception, but a fact. To the people the Catholicity of the Christian Church was embodied in the twin powers of Emperor and Pope, each equal, each exercising in his sphere the authority and dignity without which the one could not be universal emperor nor the other universal priest.[2]

To Charlemagne and Leo the apparent realisation of a universal Empire and Church, of which one was the world-monarch and the other the world-priest, was personally advantageous. Henceforth the cause of Charlemagne must be the cause of Christendom; to be his enemy was to be in schism; henceforth, too, the rights of the Church were the

[1] Selborne, *Ancient Facts and Fictions concerning Churches and Tithes*, pp. 50, 51.

[2] 'As they could not imagine, nor value if they had imagined, a communion of the saints without its expression in a Visible Church, so in matters temporal they recognised no brotherhood of spirit without the bonds of form, no universal humanity save in the image of a universal State.'—Bryce, *The Holy Roman Empire*, p. 98.

rights which the world would enforce. Each was the complement of the other. The empire of Charlemagne was no longer a collection of states won by the sword of his fathers or of himself; it was the empire of the Christian world. The diocese of the Bishop of Rome, on the other hand, was no longer southern Italy, but the broad realms over which the sword of the Emperor waved. From this time onwards, therefore, we may say the civil law superseded any merely spiritual admonitions as to the payment of tithes. Their payment was no longer a religious duty alone—it was a legal obligation, enforceable by the laws of the civil head of Christendom.

When this mediæval theory is understood, the history of tithes becomes comprehensible. Much ingenuity has been wasted on considerations whether they were due *jure divino* or not; and although Selden expressly disavows any intention of dealing with such controversial questions, many curious pieces of misguided ingenuity will be found in his citations.[1] For us it will be sufficient that, until five years after Charlemagne, as Patricius Romanorum, freed Rome from the fear of King Desiderius of Lombardy, there was no civil law in Christendom as to payment of tithes; and until 800, the same year in which he became Roman Emperor, the law did not apply to the whole of his dominions. Thenceforward, apart from any ecclesiastical theories, the payment of tithes was part of the law of the Christian world.

In 829 the payment of tithes was made enforceable by distraint both by the Emperor Louis the Simple and by Lothair for Lombardy. The means for dealing with defaulters was, first, by priestly admonition; then (in the words of Lord Selborne) by exclusion from the Church; then by the intervention of the civil power and the infliction of fines; then by a sort of interdict against defaulters' houses; and last, if the

[1] For some 'cabalistic and doting curiosities,' as Selden well styles them, see *Historie of Tithes* (1618 ed.), pp. 7, 8.

[2] Selborne, p. 54.

use of all those means failed to produce the desired effect, by bringing the offenders in custody before the imperial or royal courts.

It will have been noted that Charlemagne directed the tithes to be paid to the bishops. There were then no parishes in our modern sense, and at all events it had long been the practice of the Church that the funds contributed for the support of religion should be distributed by the bishop who was recognised as entitled to receive them.

Such funds were, according to Roman custom from at least the time of Pope Gelasius, 501, divided into four portions. One the bishop retained for himself and those who were dependent upon his hospitality; a second portion was distributed by him among his clergy; a third was administered for the benefit of the poor and strangers, and the fourth went towards maintaining the fabric of the churches. In 801 a quadripartite division was established for Lombardy by Charlemagne, and it was adopted generally in Gaul and in Germany; in Spain, however, the bishop took one-third of the whole fund, at the same time himself undertaking the repair of the churches—at least from A.D. 516, the date of the Council of Tarragona; and there are evidences that in some districts of France and the Low Countries in the ninth century (exclusive, however, of the metropolitan diocese of Paris and of Orleans) tithes were divided into three portions, one going to the Church, one to the poor, and one to the priests.[1]

In each bishopric there were generally several Mother Churches or Baptismal Churches, known under that name because, as Lord Selborne (who calls the districts attached to such churches and their dependent chapels, 'subdioceses') has observed,[2] such a church contained a baptistery where alone, except in cases of emergency, baptism could be

---

[1] As to the revenues of the episcopal treasuries and their distribution on the Continent in mediæval times, see Selborne, pp. 27-45.
[2] *Ibid.* p. 57.

administered. To the bishop the tithes were originally payable, but it was not long until questions arose between the bishop and such churches as to the right of the former to receive all the revenue and himself administer it. Even in Charlemagne's times the ordinance of 778-9 seems to have required modification, for by his Capitular *de villis* in 800, while guarding the rights of the bishops, he provided that 'if by gifts of kings or other good and God-fearing men, anything from which the older churches had been accustomed to receive tithes, under ancient titles, should have been granted to bishoprics or monasteries, the earlier gift or devotion should continue in force, and the tithes should be paid by those in possession of the land.'[1]

One of the most serious obstacles to the continuance of the ancient system of payment of tithes to the bishop was the founding by private donors of private chapels, which, as wealth increased and zeal for religion spread, were erected upon the donor's own lands, and endowed either with lands and their revenues or with the tithes of certain lands. The localising of tithes was a thing virtually unknown. Payment of tithe was both a religious and a civil duty, but it was not a local duty until lay-founders led the way by their arbitrary appropriations. The priests of such chapels were in a different position from the mission priests sent out by bishops to stations and paid by the bishops. The preachers under the bishop had no distinct parochial position. It was different when lay-founders took to appointing local priests. Against all the canon law, foundations in which the lay patron retained the property of the chapel became common; and curious scandals arose, such as the division of a church among co-heirs of such a founder; and the unseemly spectacle of three or four priests, the nominees of the three or four co-proprietors, struggling round a single altar, was not unknown. Charlemagne in 804 allowed any man to build a church on his own

[1] Selborne, p. 62.

ground, with the bishop's consent, but provided that this should not interfere with the right of the older churches to receive their tithes. Such a law shows that the bishops' pretensions to receive the whole tithe had not been well received. Public opinion is generally ahead of statute law in matters of social or religious reform, and in all probability the development of local districts is most effectually illustrated by the necessity which immediately arose of modifying Charlemagne's rule as to payment of bishops. By 816 the parochial system had grown, for by the ordinances of the Council of Aix-la-Chapelle it was required that priests should not be appointed or removed by lay-founders without the bishop's authority. While this jealousy was shown for the bishop's authority, it is impossible not to see that the ordinance recognised the necessity of not limiting the zeal of lay-founders, if only the conditions of ordinary episcopal supervision were preserved. Each church was to have a manse attached, and the tithes arising within new townships in which new churches were founded might be granted to those churches. This is virtually the birth of the parochial system; but, although in theory the parish priest has had a right to local tithes from an early date, in practice, as we shall see, it was made very difficult for him to get them.

Parishes were bound to come, sooner or later; and it was comparatively early in the modern history of the Church, as we have seen, when the parish priests, or presentees of the lay-founders of chapels with arbitrary appropriations of tithes, were admitted to have a right to such tithes as were derivable from the township in which the chapel stood. But such priests had two enemies. On the one hand, the monastic orders were constantly invading the rights of the churches which were normally founded by or in connection with the diocesan system. On the other, the laymen sometimes, instead of paying their tithes to the local priest, made gifts of churches and tithes either to monasteries or to bishops, on condition of receiving back the tithes as vassals of such bishops. Neither monks nor laymen might, canonically, hold tithes, which were the heritage of the diocesan clergy; and a synod of bishops met at St. Denis, near Paris, in 997, to endeavour to get back tithes that were improperly held. But Abbo, Abbot of Fleury,[1] offered a strenuous resistance; the mob broke in, and the synod separated in confusion.[2]

Such disputes between the two branches of the Church did not tend to make it easier to deal with laymen. The monastic orders were glad to receive gifts of tithes, on such terms as might be agreed upon, and to defend both the right of the donor to present them and of their houses to receive them.

The bishops, not to be outdone, were willing, while they insisted on the tithes nominally being their own, to return them to the layman under favourable conditions of feudal tenure. There was great restlessness in the mediæval Church: the monastic orders blamed the greed of the bishops; the bishops turned their finger to the vows of poverty which the monks professed, and then pointed to the great demesnes and large revenues of those 'poor sheep of Christ's flock.' Between them the Church seemed likely to lose much of her tithes, by the compacts she made with laymen as to the terms upon which tithes might be paid or even retained or collected by laymen.

At the Lateran Council of 1078 the possession of tithes by

[1] Selborne, p. 65.

[2] Again, as the orders settled down and acquired lands they advanced claims to immunity from payment of tithe for such lands. Hadrian IV., who ascended the papal throne in 1154, limited such exemptions, which were a fertile source of dispute, to the Cistercians, Templars, and Hospitallers; and the Lateran Council of 1215 still further confined it to lands acquired prior to that date. The exemptions were chiefly limited, however, in practice to the Templars and Hospitallers.—Selden, pp. 121, 122. See *infra*, pp. 30, 31.

laymen, whether received from bishops or kings or any other person, was declared to be sacrilege, and their restoration was demanded. The canon was admirable in its comprehensiveness, but the number of Councils in mediæval times shows how very little binding effect most of their canons had upon the Christian world in general; this canon, at least, was unworkable, and Pope Urban II. in his turn found it necessary, for the sake of peace and to avoid scandal, to confirm the holding of tithes by lay persons as such rights then existed, but he prohibited the creation of such rights in future without the bishop's consent. The Council of Poictiers in 1100 denounced the action of bishops who created such feudal holdings; Alexander III., confirming a canon of the Council of Tours in 1163, decreed that any bishop granting tithes to a layman should be deposed; and at last, at the third Lateran Council, in 1179, we come to a canon which was intended emphatically to end the matter.

The time was not unsuitable. Here again we pass a milestone in the Church's highway through history. In 779 the Church was leaning on the arm of the State. The year 800 saw the recognition of the absolute equality of Pope and Emperor, each in his sphere. But much happened in the three hundred and fifty years which followed. The Empire had fallen among Charlemagne's sons, had risen afresh under Otto, and had been degraded by Henry IV. It is in the very year that followed the Emperor's penance at Canossa that the second Lateran Council declared in unambiguous terms the Church's position towards laymen. The third Council only takes up the tale when it provides, 'We forbid laymen, detaining tithes at their soul's peril, to transfer the title to them, by any means, to others; and if any one shall receive, and not restore them to the Church, let him be deprived of Christian burial.'[1]

The Church had grown strong while the Empire had

[1] Selborne, p. 68.

wavered. The Pope now claimed an authority over the Emperor which Charlemagne might with ease have asserted over the Pope. In the see-saw of history the clergy and the laity had changed places. The Church called in the aid of the Emperor to ensure payment of ecclesiastical revenue to her bishops; the successors of those bishops are now restrained by an ecclesiastical Council from having any dealings as to such revenues with laymen.

Before the end of the twelfth century the right of parish churches on the Continent to tithes was so general that 'the burden of proof was thrown upon those claiming against them.'[1]

It is not necessary that we should follow further the history of Continental tithes. We have seen their development, from the days when a merely religious duty of paying them was known, to their legal enforcement. We have pointed out that their payment was in the early days of the Empire due only to the bishops, and that the delimiting of parishes and the recognition of a local priest's right to local teinds were matters which it took some centuries to determine.

[1] Selborne, p. 93.

CHAPTER II

TITHES IN ENGLAND, 970 TO 1066

ENGLAND was the first country outside of what was to be the Holy Roman Empire of Charlemagne which became Christian as a country. Before the end of the seventh century its conquest by Christianity was complete, and it was only a question of time when the observance of payment of tithe would become in England, as in the Empire, a civil as well as a religious duty. In England too, as on the Continent, bishoprics long preceded parishes; and how those bishoprics were determined is an interesting proof of the fact that, despite changes of the most revolutionary kind, England in her political and religious policy has preserved territorial boundaries, and specially designated districts, with marked conservatism. The limits of a diocese in early times answered commonly to those of a kingdom or principality. 'The supremacy of Kent at the beginning of the conversion,' says Freeman,[1] 'the supremacy of Northumberland at the stage when Christianity was first preached to the northern English (627), is still shown to this day in the metropolitan position of Canterbury, the city of the Bretwalda Æthelberht, and of York, the city of the Bretwalda Eadwine.' Indeed, the place-names of England are a very museum of historical relics if only we take them the right way.

For the same reasons which led us to pass very rapidly

[1] *Norman Conquest*, i. p. 29.

over the history of the tithes on the Continent prior to Charlemagne, we may pass almost unnoticed the alleged recognition of the legality of payment of tithes prior to the reign of the English Charlemagne, Edgar the Peaceful. Precepts, however, ascribed to Archbishop Theodore, but at all events written after 690, direct 'that no priest is bound to pay tithes,' 'that local custom in regard to gifts to the Church should be observed,' and 'that it is not lawful to give tithes except to the poor, and strangers or laymen to their own churches' (*sivi laici suas ad ecclesias*).[1]

Considering that there were many Englishmen at the Court of Charlemagne, and that the communication between the Emperor's Court and England was constant for centuries, it is probable that the duty of paying tithe was well understood from an early period. But there was no civil law as to the appropriation of tithes before Edgar's reign, when for seventeen years there was almost unbroken peace over the whole island. Three years before that pageant on the Dee which seems to be beyond historic doubt—when eight vassal kings rowed the king's barge under the walls of Chester—and which so admirably typified the unity and peace of his kingdom, Edgar (in 970) enacted, by the first article of his ecclesiastical ordinance made at Andover, 'That God's churches be entitled to every right; and that every tithe be rendered to the old minster to which the district belongs; and be so paid, both from a thane's in-land (*i.e.* land in the lord's hands), and from geneat-land (*i.e.* land granted out for service), so as the plough traverses it.'

The second article qualifies this right. 'But if there be any thane who on his bocland (*i.e.* his private estate) has a church at which there is a burial-place, let him give the third part of his own tithe to his church. If any one have a church at which there is not a burial-place, then, of the nine parts, let him give to his priest what he will; and let every church-

[1] Selborne, p. 107.

scot go to the old minster, according to every free health; and let plough-alms be paid when it shall be fifteen days over Easter.'

The third runs thus: 'And let a tithe of every young be paid by Pentecost; and of the fruits of the earth by the equinox, and every church-scot by Martinmass, on peril of the full "wite" which the doom-book specifies; and if any one will not then pay the tithe, as we have ordained, let the king's reeve go thereto, and the bishop's, and the mass-priest of the minster, and take by force a tenth part for the minster to which it is due; and assign to him the ninth part; and let the eight parts be divided into two, and let the landlord take possession of half, half the bishop; be it a king's man, be it a thane's.'[1]

The foundation of churches and the appointment of priests by lay-founders led to this abuse, that when the cure became vacant it was not necessarily filled up. The tithes in the meantime might well remain in the founder's hands, for the bishop had no power to interfere. At the third Lateran Council, however (1179-80), at which four English bishops were present,[2] it was settled that upon the lapse of private patronage the right to appoint devolved upon the bishop. This direction was not, of course, binding by the law of England; but it was gradually adopted, and with it the modern parochial system became established.[3]

As with Charlemagne the Empire was at its greatest before it sank in disorder, so with Edgar the unity of England passed away for many a day; but Canute—who was certainly the greatest legislator prior to the Conquest—re-enacted Edgar's law about tithe, with other laws, about 1018-21. The troubles which overtook England between 975 and 1020, a period of forty-five years, prevented anything like the development of ecclesiastical and parochial

[1] Thorpe's *Ancient Laws*, 1840, i. pp. 263-5.
[2] Selden, p. 388.   [3] Selborne, p. 295.

government which might have been expected. England started well on its progress as a Christian Power; but the troubles with invaders who were but half-Christian, and the weakness of the native kings, prevented any steady or civil recognition of ecclesiastical territorial divisions, much less of a strict law of tithes. The laws of both Edgar and Canute, however, are valuable, not only for what they say, but for what they do not say. When Edgar provides for a certain portion of the tithes being paid to the manorial church, it is sufficiently clear that there were not only baptismal churches, but churches of a semi-parochial character upon manors, and that there had been doubts as to the right of tithe-payers to withhold any portion of their tithe from the bishop's church and devote it to dependent chapels.

Parochia was acquiring a new meaning just as it had done on the Continent. The evidence that in England, as abroad, it had originally meant a diocese and nothing more, is, as Selden says,[1] very obvious both in Latin and in Saxon. Two instances will perhaps suffice (in Selden's words): 'It is related,' he says, 'of King Cenwalh [660] that he divided *Provinciam in duas Parochia*, when he made a new Bishoprique at Winchester that was taken out of the Diocese of Dorchester. And in the Council of Hertford held under Theodore, Archbishop of Canterburie, one canon is *Ut nullus Episcoparum Parochiam alterius invadat sed contentus sit gubernatione creditæ sibi plebis.*'

Yet districts had been assigned to local churches for the convenience of both priests and people, although there was no obligation on the people to confine their devotion or their gifts to the church which happened to be near their residence, nor did the clergy of the districts reside within their districts. Their general place of abode was the bishop's house, and their maintenance was from the fund apportioned out of the tithe payable to the baptismal church for the service of which they

[1] Selden, p. 257.

were ordained. The appearance of the priests in public, indeed, from Bede's account, was in early times very rare; 'so rarely were they seen abroad that whenever any of them were espied in the country, the people used presently to flock about him, and with all reverence humbly to beseech his Benison, either by signing them with the Crosse, or in holy prayers for them; and with all earnestness of attention they heard what he preached. How long this communitie in every Diocese between the bishop and the attending clergie continued, fully appears not. But, that it was not out of use till past more then c yeers after Augustine's comming, that is till past DCC years from Christ, may be conjectured out of those testimonies of Bede which extend as farre.' Thus Selden.

The early Church, then, was essentially non-parochial. It was not, however, so purely an Episcopal Church as that of the primitive Church in Italy. The theory of the Church was the same, but the rise of the orders early introduced a new element into the English Church's economy. To discuss the relative position of the secular clergy and of the regular clergy[1] would be foreign to the purpose of this summary, but it is necessary that it should be remembered that there were two monastic movements in the Church.

[1] The words Secular and Regular have so entirely changed their meaning that it is necessary to remind the reader that the Secular clergy were the clergy pertaining to the Episcopate, or non-monastic; the Regular clergy were the members of the religious orders who lived under special regulations of the founders. Thus, to take a modern illustration, the officers of the Salvation Army from a mediæval point of view might be regarded as Regulars, while the Archbishop of Canterbury is certainly one of the Secular clergy. The word Regular in ecclesiastical phraseology has, in fact, made a complete somersault.

We have perhaps an illustration of the distaste of the Secular clergy for the Regulars in one of the *Exempla* of Jacques de Vitry, Bishop of Acre, 1214, when he tells of two brothers, one of whom was brought up in a monastery and the other in the world. When the two attained majority, 'plures civillationes et dolos scivit claustralis et multo magis maliciosus fuit quam qui in seculo remansit.' (*Exempla*, ed. by Crane, 1890, p. 19.)

Augustine, the apostle of English Christianity, was a monk, but of the system of primitive monasticism; and Gregory's directions to him were that, although trained as a monk, he ought not to live separately from his clergy, but should institute an English Church conforming so far as possible to the administration of the early Church. Augustine, therefore, did not found a Benedictine monastery, but collected around him a college for clergy, the germ of the chapter of Canterbury Cathedral, although subsequently to Dunstan's time its organisation was altered.

The monasteries were, as we have seen, the residences of the clergy; and all priests, whether in colleges or in monasteries, were directly under the bishop of the *parochia*. Some of the houses which were known as monasteries were scarcely more than asylums, places of retirement, as Stubbs says, for worn-out statesmen and for public functionaries—kings, queens, and ealdormen, 'whose forced seclusion gave to their retreats somewhat of the character of reformatories.'[1] Some of them in Bede's time were already too rich and full of abuses, calling even in the eighth century for a reform which separated, at least nominally, the secular from the monastic clerks. In the history of some there are traces of the hereditary descent of the priesthood.[2] Some were certainly houses where both men and women were received. The early monastic houses were, indeed, very different from those of the Benedictines which Dunstan found at Ghent during his exile; and although he

[1] Stubbs, *Constitutional History of England*, i. p. 257.
[2] 'Either clerical celibacy was unknown, or the successive heads of the monasteries must have delayed ordination until they became fathers and mothers of families large enough to continue the succession' (Stubbs, i. p. 256). There is no ambiguity as to the conditions upon which Abbot Headda left his monastery to the See of Winchester: 'quod mei heredes in mea genealogia in ecclesiastico gradu de virili sexu percipiant, quamdiu in mea prosapia tam sapiens et praesciens inveniri potest qui rite et monastice ecclesiasticam normam regere queat et nunquam potestati laicorum subdetur' (*Cod. Dipl.* clxix). Theodore forbade such succession.

does not seem to have himself been a violent partisan of the new order of things, it was in his time that the regular clergy began to assert their superiority, if not their independence of the secular clergy. Without digression upon the matter it is important to bear in mind that the second monastic movement was very different from the first, because it was the independence of the new monastic houses which was undoubtedly responsible for many of the arbitrary appropriations of tithes to which reference will afterwards be made. The monks in succeeding generations taught a somewhat free doctrine as to *parochial* liability to pay tithes, so long as tithes were paid to *some* ecclesiastical body, and reaped the reward of their liberal doctrines in appropriations to their own foundations. Such teaching was abhorrent to the secular clergy.

The so-called laws of Edward the Confessor direct the payment of not only prædial, but personal tithes to the Church, but Lord Selborne considers the MS. apocryphal, 'and not to be relied upon for any historical purpose.'[1]

In the laws of William the Conqueror, however, we indirectly find the growth of parishes illustrated, for he provides that if a cathedral, or a monastery, or other religious house (*cenobium vel quæcunque religiosorum ecclesia*) is violated, the forfeiture will be 100 shillings; if 'a mother parish church' (*matrix ecclesia parochialis*), twenty shillings; if a chapel, ten shillings. This mother parish church, as Lord Selborne says, can only be Edgar's church with a burial ground. By the end of the twelfth century, there was a general presumption that every parish church was endowed with its own tithes, if they could not be proved to have been appropriated to a particular monastery, but such endowments were never made by any general law. The endowment was the result of custom. No law ever restricted local tithes to a local church up to the end of the twelfth century. The obligation to pay tithes was indeed

[1] Selborne, p. 302.

universal, but where they should be paid was a matter for the payer's choice. Thus in the Chronicle of Battle Abbey, written about 1176, the Chronicler says :

'As it was permitted up to that time [the foundation of the Abbey in 1066] for every one to pay his tithe where, or to whomsoever he would, many of those who resided in the neighbourhood assigned theirs to the Abbey in perpetuity, and these, being confirmed by episcopal authority, remain payable to the Abbey until this day.' Other instances of a century later, 1279, are cited by Selden, p. 357, and Selborne, p. 308. In 1371 Ludlow, one of King Edward III.'s Judges of Assize, said, 'Anciently every man might grant the tithe of his land to any church that he pleased.'[1]

If a lord could grant his tithes to any church, it is clear he might endow his own church, and this brings us to the *crux* of most writers on tithes, the 'arbitrary appropriations' of which Selden speaks. In the nature of things nothing seems more reasonable or more natural than that a lord of a manor should appropriate his tithes definitely to his own church. No doubt, ecclesiastically, the consent of the bishop may have been necessary to this ; but the founder had it in his power to make his bargain with the bishop before he undertook to erect his church. There was thus, as Lord Selborne has said, two minds to the contract ; and, once made, there was no reason why the carrying out of the bargain should not have been insisted upon by the founder, and the parish in its first ecclesiastical form grew out of the manor. As time passed on, and churches increased, the ecclesiastical district became practically identical with the ancient township ; it is the ancient *vicus* or

---

[1] The stages of progress may be stated thus :—690, Ina, king of Wessex, imposes penalties on those who fight in several secular buildings, which he names, or in a mynstre (minster), or monastery ; evidently there was no other recognised public church. 970, Edgar speaks of the 'old minster,' and the manorial church. 1066, we have (1) William's 'minster,' (2) the mother parish church, originally manorial, (3) chapels afterwards to develop into local parish churches.

tun-scipe regarded ecclesiastically. Many of the townships were too small to support a separate church and priest, so one parish might contain several townships, 'but the fact of a township lying partly in one parish and partly in another, without being very uncommon, is rare enough,' says Bishop Stubbs, 'to be exceptional, and may generally be accounted for by more recent history.'[1]

We have seen how the civil obligation to pay tithes, instituted by Charlemagne, was recognised in England as the circumstances of the time permitted; that bishoprics, as on the Continent, long preceded parishes; that parishes were the result of the widening out of the Church's work, that the tithes, which originally were payable to bishops, were gradually appropriated to the clergy of such parishes, and it has been indicated that while the early Church was got into shape by the secular clergy, there was, subsequent to the time of Dunstan, a marked advance of the new regular clergy, who were not parochial or necessarily diocesan, and whose interest it was for the benefit of their religious houses to encourage appropriation of tithes either to parochial churches or to themselves, for religious purposes which might be parochial or which might not.[2] It is not necessary that the history of tithes in England should detain us longer, for it was at the point, reached about the time of the Norman Conquest, that the religious system then developed, or in course of development, was imported

[1] *Constitutional History*, i. p. 260.
[2] We find instances of churches which were both parochial and monastic. Thus Dunster church in Somersetshire was, after 1499, double, one church being used by the vicar of the parish, and the other by the neighbouring priory of Benedictines. The Benedictine portion is now in ruins. Again Davington Priory was originally two churches under one roof, the western portion being the church of the Benedictine Sisters of Davington, the eastern portion, that of the vicar of the parish. In this case, it is the parochial portion of the building which has long been distroyed. Sherborne Minster was also partly monastic, partly parochial. See *Notes and Queries*, 8th S. iii. pp. 257-8.

into Scotland by Queen Margaret, the niece of the Confessor, and the many English gentlemen who followed the Atheling and his sister to the court of Malcolm Canmore. The change in the history of Scotland at this point is, indeed, from a social point of view, startling, for when we read of St. Margaret and of Turgot, it is difficult to believe that the Queen's immediate predecessor on the Scottish throne was the Lady Macbeth of Shakespeare.

CHAPTER III

TITHES IN SCOTLAND BEFORE THE REFORMATION: 1058-1560

WE have now traced the development of the civil recognition of the religious obligation to pay tithes, and the growth of the parochial idea.

We have seen how the influence of Charlemagne, whose adviser was so generally the English Alcuin, reacted upon England, even under Danish kings. The English Church passed through three stages, the early monastic, the almost purely secular, and the secular and new monastic. It was in the first that the Christian Church in England began; it was in the second that Edgar gave his law as to tithes; it was in the third that the Conqueror re-enacted the laws of his Saxon predecessors.

Where does the Scottish law custom of tithes-paying begin?

Sir John Connell says that 'the existence of tithes in Scotland, prior to the time of David I., and their establishment during the reign of that monarch, are fully proved.' This statement is perhaps rather too general.

It is true that grants were made to religious houses at a very early date. So early as the ninth century Cyric (the 'Grig' of Connell, whose name is perpetuated in Cyruskirk = Eccles Grig) transferred the privileges of Dunkeld, which itself had succeeded Abernethy, the heir of Iona, to the church of St. Andrews, and the historical Macbeth and his queen (1040-1058) were among the benefactors of the Culdee priory of

Lochleven; such grants were numerous. It is also true that the first Scottish parish, that of Ednam in Roxburghshire, was created by Thor the Long, in the reign of William I., King David's brother and predecessor, and that tithes are referred to in a document of David's reign, as having been given to the chapel of Stirling by Alexander, to which we shall again refer; but one swallow does not make a spring; the establishment at Ednam was exceptional, and the tithes of Alexander's times seem to have been a royal gift and nothing more.

There is no proof that tithes, or anything like the payment of tithes, was *ordinarily* recognised as a civil obligation for long after the time of Alexander. He and his brothers, brought up under the influence of an English mother and of a very English court, were early acquainted with the practice of England; but Scotland was in no condition, in Alexander's time, to render the obligation of general tithe-paying possible. Nor was it in David's reign.

Connell speaks of the 'existence of tithes *in Scotland*,' and his words might lead the reader to suppose that Alexander was King of Scotland in the sense in which the later Stuarts were kings; but this, of course, he was not. Up to the accession of David, while the royal authority extended practically as far north as the Spey,[1] the country between the Forth, the Tay, and the central ridge of the Grampian range was the real home and centre of Alban. David was Prince of Cumbria, and with his accession Southern Scotland began to develop, but even in his time the Lord of Galloway was rather an ally than a vassal, and was indeed married to a natural daughter of Henry I. of England, David's brother-in-law. The kingdom of the Isles was under the Scandinavian crown. All, therefore, that remains of Connell's statement which can be historically affirmed, is that Alexander, while king of a portion of modern Scotland, recognised the duty of paying tithes in certain instances. Even had he wished to make tithes obli-

[1] Robertson, *Scotland under her Early Kings*, i. p. 232.

gatory, he could not have done so; and looking at the ecclesiastical difficulties between the Culdees and the Anglican Church in the reign of David, it is not doubtful that that sovereign only established the payment of tithes to the extent of making grants of land under burden of tithes, or of making grants of tithes, or confirming such grants to the houses of the clergy who derived their orders from the English Church, *not* that he regarded such tithes as payable, as a matter of course, for the maintenance of the ordinary or parochial clergy, which, at least at the beginning of his reign, would have meant the endowment of the Culdees, with their non-canonical Easter, distinctive tonsure, and tribal rather than territorial basis—a thing very far from his intentions. Tithe-paying, as the English Church of the time understood it, too, was utterly foreign to the Culdee theory of church maintenance.

The state of things in St. Andrews at David's accession will illustrate this. The college of Kilrimont, or St. Andrews, was served by a prior and twelve Culdees, of whom five never officiated at the altar. The remaining seven seem to have had each his chapel, and the offerings at each chapel were divided into seven, one going to the bishop, one to the hospital—the invariable appendage of a Culdee monastery—and the five lay-Culdees (if we may so call them) received the rest, on condition of maintaining pilgrims when the hospital, which held six, was full. The Culdee houses were nearly always made up of members of the same family, the leading one of the neighbourhood, or that of the founder, and in this case they seem to have been connected with the Comyns.[1]

King David's reforming work was as thorough as it was speedy, and the Culdee Church was practically superseded by his efforts,[2] but for the reasons we have given, it is in the

---

[1] Robertson, pp. i. 337-339.

[2] Strangely enough, one Culdee house, that of Kirkheugh, survived, with prior and twelve prebendaries, at the time of the Reformation.—Robertson, i. p. 344.

highest degree improbable that in his time the establishment of tithes can be 'fully proved.' He led the way, and the Church was glad to follow. It would probably be correct to say that from and after the reign of King David, when feudalism burst into flower, in Scotland with more speed than probably in any other country, the duty of paying tithes was generally recognised, and the law of England as to tithe-granting and tithe-collecting was by the influence of the clergy under the new church discipline as rapidly as possible introduced into the practice of Scotland. In David's principality of Cumbria the work was easier for him than elsewhere, because the Culdees seem never to have been established south of the Forth, and therefore it was natural that in that fertile land the foundation and endowment of ecclesiastical houses were speedier than elsewhere. How far David was from associating churches specially with their localities is shown by his gift of the patronage of the Priory of May in the Forth to the Monastery of Reading in England. Alexander III. re-acquired the right of purchase. The See of Dunblane, on the other hand, long nominally enjoyed the lordships of Appleby, Troclyngham, Congere, and Malemath, though the bishop's rights would have been somewhat difficulty to enforce in later years. We take up, in fact, in David's reign, the theory of tithes as it existed at the court of his granduncle, Edward the Confessor. Tithe-paying is regarded as a duty, but certainly the maxim, *decimæ debentur parocho*, was not understood by David or his predecessors, or was regarded only as a maxim, not as a precept to be acted upon, for long afterwards.

As a specimen of King David's grants, we may take the gift to the Priory of St. Andrews of the church of St. Mary of Haddington, with all the chapels, lands, rights, and customs belonging to it within the shire of Haddington, free from the King, the thane, and all who held of the King or the freeholders of the shire. The tithes were attached to the Kirktown, which was also donated, the effect being that they might be alienated from the church by the Persona who held the Kirktown. Aberdeen bishopric received 'the whole vill of old Aberdeen, and the church of the Kirktown, with the shire of Clat, the shire of Tulinestyn, the shire of Rayn, and the shire of Daviot, with their pertinents and churches, and the tithes of the rents of the thanages and escheats within the sheriffdoms of Aberdeen and Banff.'[1] There is no trace of parishes here; the favoured church was usually endowed evidently with thanages equal to the early English shire, a district reckoned at twelve townships, and eight-and-forty ploughlands, or davochs. But it may be that in the thanages we have the germ of the parish. It should perhaps be noted that the word Kirktown in succeeding centuries ceased to mean the township belonging to the minster, and carrying tithes, and as a designation was transferred to the carucate or half-carucates of land made over as glebe to a vicarage.[2]

David had enough to do in dividing the country into bishoprics without seeking to secure a compulsory recognition of parishes. He found four bishoprics, those of Glasgow, St. Andrews, Dunkeld, and Moray, but in two of them the old abbacies had become appanages of the royal family.[3] He left behind him five new bishoprics, viz., Dunblane, Brechin, Aberdeen, Ross, and Caithness, but of some of them the chapter must have been little more than nominal.[4] Dunblane and Brechin were probably formed out of the remains of the old Pictish bishopric of Abernethy.

As illustrating the want of sufficient geographical boundaries to church lands, the case of the Crags of Gorgie may be referred to. Ethelred, one of the sons of Malcolm Canmore, towards the end of the eleventh century, presented the church and lands of St. Cuthbert's, Hales, or Colinton, to the Dunfermline Abbey, or rather to its predecessor the Church

---

[1] Robertson, *Historical Essays*, pp. 126, 127.   [2] *Ibid.* p. 128.
[3] Robertson, *Early Kings*, i. p. 334.   [4] Skene, *Celtic Scotland*, ii. p. 397.

of the Holy Trinity. David I., who was a younger brother of Ethelred, about 1128, presented the church and lands of St. Cuthbert's, Edinburgh, with other churches and lands, to the Abbey of Holyrood. Within a century later a vigorous dispute arose between Dunfermline Abbey and the rector of Hales acting together, and the abbot of Holyrood, as to the teinds of the Craggs of Gorgie, which the one claimed to be in the lands of St. Cuthbert, Hales, and the other of St. Cuthbert's, Edinburgh. The dispute was compromised under the authority of the abbot of Lindores and the prior of St. Andrews, acting 'with the mandate of the Pope,' Dunfermline renouncing its rights to the teinds in question, on condition that 'for the sake of peace' Holyrood should give each year one bezant, or two shillings at Martinmas, towards providing lights in the church of St. Cuthbert at Hales. Probably the sum to be thus paid was about equal to the surrendered teinds.[1]

There is one good historical definition of tithes, more or less parochial, in early times which should not be omitted. A dispute arose between the royal chapel of Stirling Castle and the parish church of Eccles, within which the Castle stood, and it was decided, in presence of King David, *apud castellum puellarum*, not in an ecclesiastical tribunal. Evidence was given that when King Alexander dedicated the Castle chapel he granted to it the tithes of his demesnes in the soke of Stirling whether they should increase or decrease. The lords decided 'that the parish church of Eccles ought to have all the tithes paid by the Hurdmen and Bonds and Gresmen with the other dues which they owe to the church; and that whoever died, whether of the demesne lands, or of the parish, their bodies should lie in the parish cemetery, with such things as the dead ought to have with them to the church; unless by chance any of the burghers die there suddenly . . .

[1] 'The Teinds *De Craggis et Gorgin*,' by the Rev. W. Lockhart, *Proceedings of the Socy. of Antiq. of Scotland*, vol. xxi. pp. 275 *et seq.*

and if the demesnes shall increase by grubbing out of wood or breaking up of land not tilled before, the chapel shall have the tithes ... and if the number of men of the demesne increase, the tithes of them and of all who cultivate it shall go to the chapel; and the parish church shall have their bodies.'[1] This anxious delimitation of the parish rights was, however, of course, due to the proximity of the royal chapel, and its careful organisation must have been merely an islet in a sea of irregular ecclesiastical constitutions. It was only with regard to parishes under the shadow and protection of royal castles that such regulations as are above cited could be made, and I cannot regard the case as illustrating ordinary knowledge of parochial requirements. On the contrary, the parish of Eccles seems to me to have been exceptional and remarkable to the men of David's time, hence the solemn council to decide as to what Alexander exactly meant by his royal gift *more Anglicano* of tithes.

By the end of the reign of William the Lion, David's grandson, the powers of a Scottish king had been greatly consolidated. The general payment of tithes was enforced throughout the kingdom. William founded the monastery of Arbroath, dedicating it to Thomas à Becket, with whose contests with the English king his own career had been so strangely associated, and gave it 'Aberbrothoc with the whole shire,' and various miscellaneous endowments such as a net's fishing in Tay, called Stok, and one in the North Esk; a salt-work in the Carse of Stirling; the ferryboat of Montrose, with its land; and the patronage and tithes of at least twenty-two churches.[2]

The Abbey of Inchaffray was endowed by its charter of 1200 with five churches, and with the tithe of the founder (the Earl of Fife), kain, and rents of wheat, meal, malt, cheese, and all provisions used year by year in his court, tithe of

---

[1] Innes, *Early Scottish History*, p. 16.   [2] *Ibid.* p. 146.

all fish brought into his kitchen, tithe of his hunting, and tithe of the profits of his courts of justice.[1]

William tried to improve the sees of Aberdeen and Moray, but Brechin and Dunblane still remained little more than nominal bishoprics for the Church lands were in the hands of laymen.

The term parish, which, as we have seen, at first meant a bishopric, in Scotland came to mean first the territory of a baptismal church, the 'minster' of England, and subsequently, by the middle of the thirteenth century, a parish in its modern signification, more or less, the words *parochia et parochiani* being used much in their present sense;[2] and the district of the mother church, which Selborne calls a sub-diocese, was known as Plebania.[3]

A map illustrating the state of the Church in the reign of David I. is given by Skene;[4] the bishopric of Caithness, however, which is there shown, he admits to have had 'little reality,'[5] as Caithness was in the possession of the Norwegian Earl of Orkney,[6] and there is no doubt that the development of parishes followed the same lines in Scotland as in England, arising out of the bishoprics, with their baptismal churches. Probably more rapidly than in England came monasteries and manorial churches, both forces tending towards decentralisation; and it should not be forgotten that while the Culdee Church was reformed it was not entirely suppressed, and in

---

[1] Innes, *Early Scottish History*, p. 209.   [2] *Ibid.* p. 2.

[3] 'Of this kind was Stobo, with its four subordinate parishes of Broughton, Dawie, Drummelyier, and Tweedsmuir, where the parson was styled Dean, and was, it would seem, in very early times, hereditary, like some of the heads of the regular convents.' *Regist. Glasg.*; Innes, *Early Scottish History*, p. 3, note.

[4] *Celtic Scotland*, vol. ii., facing p. 418.   [5] *Ibid.* p. 383.

[6] Many appropriations of churches, etc., by David, in which the authority of the bishops as in the early English Church will be found in Connell's work. See as to his many pious foundations, Bellesheim's *History of the Catholic Church in Scotland*.

every group of Culdee cells there was the germ of parochial organisation. The actual mapping-out of parishes was a very slow thing—the work of centuries.

That the duty of paying tithes was understood generally in the reign of Alexander II. is illustrated in the report of the murder of Adam, bishop of Caithness, who it appears was over rigorous in exacting tithes; but as the bonders of Caithness's chief grievance was that Adam at the instigation of a monk named Serlo had *doubled* his exactions, we also learn from this incident what lax notions the clergy entertained as to what was their legal due.[1]

In the time of Alexander III. the great religious houses usually gave one-third of the tithes to the vicars.[2] In his reign the ancient kingdom of the Isles was made over to the Scottish Crown, with the patronage of the bishopric, reserving the ecclesiastical rights of the Archbishop of Drontheim.[3]

How soon Scotland might have settled down into a rich, well-governed, well-taught nation, another England, a survival of the kingdom of Edgar reappearing north of the Forth, with most of its nobility of Anglo-Saxon origin, we can only speculate; history shows us how speedily the Wars of the Succession threw our land back into semi-barbarism. When regular warfare between England and Scotland began to render settled life in the Lowlands impossible, the Anglo-Saxon nobles retired, and Norman England received again the descendants of the men who had followed the fortunes of the Atheling and Queen Margaret. The native lords regained in large measure the position they had lost under the firm rule of Malcolm Canmore and his sons.

Scotland presents for many centuries a melancholy picture, not only as regards her politics, but also in respect to her ecclesiastical organisation.

There was much litigation between the various religious foundations as to tithes and lands to which they had acquired

---

[1] Robertson, ii. pp. 18, 19.   [2] *Ibid.* p. 138.   [3] *Ibid.* p. 105.

rights. Such disputes were generally settled by Rome, except in the case of the abbots of Melrose, Dryburgh, Jedburgh, and Kelso, who established a rule that when any difference arose between two of the monasteries, the other two should act as arbiters, and thus save the cost of Roman litigation.[1] The Culdees, such as survived, took small part in the suits, which were generally waged between a bishop and a religious order. As in England, the regular clergy had become very powerful; and their doctrine as regarded tithes was so loose as to call down the censure of Innocent IV. in 1250, who calls those who, like the Dominicans and Franciscans, taught that tithes might be disposed of in charity as a man pleased, *isti novi magistri et prædicatores qui docent et prædicant contra Novum et Vetus Testamentum.* The Council of Verona condemned this teaching in 1340, and in England, one William Russell, a Franciscan, who preached the pernicious doctrine—which was supposed, rightly, to be most to the benefit of the begging friars—was condemned in Convocation, and ordered to recant on a fixed day at Paul's Cross; he fled the kingdom, and was pronounced a heretic, and his opinions were condemned by both Oxford and Cambridge Universities.[2]

---

[1] Innes, *Early Scottish History*, p. 115.

[2] Of the ordinary or orthodox teaching as to tithes in the Middle Ages, Selden gives the following curious example from 'a Penitential Mode for Direction of Priests in Auricular Confession, and written (as my Copie is) about Henrie the sixth, the Priests examination and advise upon the point of Tithing is thus expressed:—" Hast thou truly doo thy Tithings and Offrings to God and to holichirch? thou shalt understande that at the beginning of the worlde, whan ther was but oo man, that is to say, Adam, God chargyd him that he sholde truly of al maner thyng give God the xth parte, and bad hym that he sholde teche his children to doo the same maner, and so forthe al men into the worldis ende. And forasmuch as ther was that tyme no man to receive it of hem in the name of holichirche, and God wolde not that thei sholde have but ix parties. Therefor he commandid hem that of every thyng the Tithe parte should be brent. I

When they did not teach that tithe was merely charity, the Orders took up the other position, that as being the poor of Christ's flock, they were not liable in payment of tithes for such lands as they had come to possess. Ultimately the exception was limited to the Cistercians, Knights Templar, and Knights Hospitallers, and but a limited exception was allowed to other Orders in respect of such lands—*novalia*—as they might themselves have brought under cultivation, so long as the land remained in their hands; but tithe became payable if such lands were leased. It was by the influence of monasticism that in Scotland, as Innes says, 'the goodly framework of a parochial establishment was shipwrecked when scarcely formed.'[1] A useful list of religious Orders in Scotland is given at the end of Spotswood's *History*; the distinction between monks and friars should be noted—it was the begging friars who were most objectionable to the laymen of the Middle Ages.

The possessions of the excepted Orders, particularly of the Knights Hospitallers or Knights of St. John of Jerusalem, tended very much to run in family lines, which almost remind us of the hereditary semi-laic, semi-clerical establishment of the Culdees.

An evidence of the close connection between the head of

fynd that afterward Adam had two sonnes, Caime and Abell, Abell tithed truly and of the best. Caym tythed falsely and of the werst: at last the fals Tyther Cayme slough Abell his brother, for he blamyd hym and seyd that he tythed evel, wherefor our Lord God accursid Caym and al the erth in his werk. So ye mow se that fals tything was the cause of the first manslaughter that ever was, and it was cause that God cursid the erthe," it is literally transcribed as I find it; that writing of *Cayme*, or *Cain*, is ordinarie in the moniments of that age, as you may find in Wickleves works, Waldensis his Doctrinal, and others of like nature.'—*Tithes*, 1618 ed., pp. 169, 170. Such teaching was probably as common in Scotland as in England.

[1] *Early Scottish History*, p. 17; see also *Scotch Legal Antiquities*, pp. 162 *et seq.*

the Order of St. John and the Livingston family of Torphichen is incidentally afforded by a tack of certain Temple lands granted in 1461 by Frere Henry of Levyngstoune, 'Knight Commander of the Order of Saint John of Jerusalem, within the kingdom of Scotland,' to his 'derraste cusings William of Levyngstone and Alisiandre of Levyngstoune, sonnys til umquhile our derraste brothir William of Levyngstone of Balcastell.'[1]

Although the monasteries succeeded in attaching to themselves the tithes which in early days were paid to the baptismal church, as they grew richer they felt it a great injustice when, although indirectly, they in turn were required to contribute to the civil power. With the sanction of Pope Alexander VI., the religious houses in England however were required to contribute towards the cost of a crusade. They resisted. 'Such a demand was unheard of,' they said. 'Hitherto the laymen had paid tithes to the Church. Now churchmen, *et inviti*, against their will, were to furnish money for knights and men-at-arms.' But their resistance was overcome by the stratagem of Peter de Egilbanke, Bishop of Hereford. On his suggestion the Pope borrowed the necessary money from Italian merchants, and granted them powers of distraint upon the abbeys which had claimed exemption.[2]

The Pope from time to time demanded payment of one-tenth of the revenues of the Scottish religious houses—a species of tithe, but rather of tithes of rents than of the produce of the soil alone, which tithes are; and he even granted this tenth for a time to the service of the King of England. Such exactions were very unpalatable to the Scottish kings,

---

[1] See 'Notice of an Original Tack of Temple Lands,' by Joseph Bain, F.S.A.Scot., *Proceedings of the Society of Antiquaries of Scotland*, xvii. pp. 312 *et seq.*

[2] Froude, 'Annals of an English Abbey' (St. Albans).—*Short Studies*, 1888, iii. pp. 46, 47.

who preferred to have the produce of taxes on monasteries themselves, and who were never friendly to the interference of foreign legates in their affairs.

It would be tedious, and here scarcely profitable, to follow step by step the growth of the Church in Scotland. It grew with the king's power, but it did not fall with the king's weakness. While the fortunes of the State rose and fell with the firm reigns or the long minorities, the Church, on the whole, progressed steadily without one backward step. Her good fortune was, indeed, her curse, for with her increasing wealth came the abuses which have accompanied ecclesiastical wealth in all ages. The tendency of a wealthy and luxurious corporation is to draw within itself persons who are ambitious of enjoying the benefits of wealth; and the Church suffered her fold to be entered, not by men possessed only by a holy desire for religion, but by those who saw the easiest and quickest way to political eminence was through the Church, and who, as statesmen, regarded the means of their rise rather as a political than as a religious organisation. We must not forget, also, that so late as the reign of William the Lion there were lay-holders of many rich Church lands on the old Culdaic foundations; so that the idea of holding Church lands was never unfamiliar to the Scottish aristocracy. Between the two sets of ideas, that of the political Churchman and that of the semi-clerical layman, the Church as a corporation took a middle course. She reconciled the latter to the idea of owning the Church's superiority by giving him the right to draw the real profits; and she made the path of the clerical politician the more easy by making it, so far as possible, the interest of such feudal lords to support those who spoke in the nation's councils in the name of the Church, rather than oppose them.

The country, when with its increasing civilisation and its wealthy Church it gradually settled into parishes, had, at least in name, the cures served by rectors, who drew the *decimæ garbales*, or teinds of corn or wheat, barley, oats, pease, etc., but more often by vicars, the substitutes and servants of the great churches which owned the tithes, who drew the lesser teinds of lamb, wool, milk, flax, cheese, and eggs. Personal teinds from the fruits of personal industry, profits of commerce, wages of labour, etc., were scarcely known in Scotland. One doubtful instance occurs in the case of *Birnie v. Brown*, Nov. 29, 1678 (M. Dict. 11,000), where the Court decerned for a yearly sum out of each weaver's loom, and for the salt made in the parish.[1] From a presumption that personal tithes had not been paid at the time of a man's death arose the custom, sanctioned by canon, of mortuaries payable in beasts, which existed in England up to 21 H. VIII. The mortuary was presented with the body at the burial, as a satisfaction for omission to pay personal tithes, and the custom was styled *corse-present*. Selden says he has seen a justification, in the Eyre of Derby of 4 Edw. III., to an action of trespass brought by Thomas of Goustill against the parson of Whitwell for taking a horse, in which the parson pleads that it was the horse of one I. Leyer, his parishioner, who had died.[2] Personal tithes, no doubt, where, as in Venice, there were no prædial tithes, were exactable; but for obvious reasons prædial tithes were in the Middle Ages much preferable to a non-enforceable income-tax, culminating in a

---

[1] The tithe paid by Abraham to Melchisedek, on which all canonists found, is described as follows:—'And he gave him a tenth of all.' What the 'all' was has been copiously considered, but common sense would suggest that it was the 'all' he had captured, *i.e.* it was *personal* teind. This view was taken in England, for *The Story of Genesis and the Exodus*, the Early English song written about 1250, tells how Abraham gave 'of alle if begete,' *i.e.* of his spoils or winnings.—Early English Text Society ed., line 806. Milton long afterwards finds it necessary to give the same reading: 'Abraham on the other side honours him with the tenth of all, that is to say (for he took not sure his whole estate with him to that war), of the spoils.'—*The Likeliest Means to remove Hirelings out of the Church*.

[2] Selden, p. 287.

death-duty, which the demand for personal tithes really amounted to.

Buchanan's statement that in Scotland the rector or parson originally did the whole duty of the benefice, and drew the whole teinds, great and small, and that it was owing to the practice of annexing churches, with their teinds, to a monastery that the institution of the vicar began,[1] is obviously incorrect, because it proceeds, as is usual with legal writers, on the assumption that Scotland's ecclesiastical organisation started parochially, and that there was an Arcadian time when every parson drew all the tithes of his parish from willing parishioners, and without any fear of monastery or bishop. This is mere dreaming, for, as we have seen, the diocese, as in England, long preceded local organisation, and groups of thaneships long preceded districts with ecclesiastical boundaries. The rector, indeed, who drew all his tithes at any time and locally, must have been a *rara avis in terra*, and only did so, probably, because he was either the younger son of some great family, or was under the special protection of some lay lord who was strong enough to see that the rector got what the heritors conceded that the law allowed him. The privileges of the clergy were cruelly restricted by the annexation of tithes to monasteries; but, on the other hand, it was by the churches founded by lay patrons and conveyed to such monasteries, and by churches founded by the monasteries themselves, that the local organisation of parishes developed.

The right of the local clergyman to receive the teinds was no doubt theoretically recognised, as for instance in a bull of Gregory IX. in 1230, which confirmed the right of the Monastery of Dryburgh to the Church of Golyn 'when it shall be vacant'—*i.e.* reserving the right of the then incumbent; but the difficulty of the local clergyman was generally to get his teinds. It is clear that when Golyn became vacant the new

---

[1] *Law of Teinds*, p. 9.

priest would have no teinds; he would require to receive a salary from Dryburgh. The local clergy were in fact, throughout Scotland, stipendiaries, or, in other words, curates-in-charge, who only received as salary what they might bargain for.

It will no doubt be observed that we have said nothing about the establishment of tithes by law in Scotland.

The explanation of this is to be found in the altered position of the Church, when settled in Scotland under David, to what it had been either in Germany in the time of Charlemagne, or in England under Edgar.

The Church was now standing by herself, and as far as possible resisted any State interference with her 'rights,' among which that of collecting teinds was undoubtedly included. It was sufficient for the Church that the right had been enunciated by the canonists, and that the sovereigns of Scotland recognised the pious duty, and were ready, if necessary, to assist in enforcing it; but to have asked the State to make by Act of Parliament the collection of tithes lawful would have seemed to the Churchmen of Hildebrand's school an extraordinary and superfluous request.

There was probably another reason for the State's early reticence as to tithes. The Papacy and the Scottish Crown were on terms of somewhat constrained friendship. The sovereigns of Scotland rather dealt with the clergy as regards tithes on the basis of custom and use and wont than otherwise.

That this use and wont included the right of bishops, or judges appointed by the Pope, to exercise a jurisdiction in relation to teinds was generally admitted, and is sufficiently proved by numerous cases.[1] In 1319, it is true, the civil rights of the Rector of Kinross regarding some lands, a servitude of pasturage, and a fishing in Lochleven, were decided

---

[1] See Connell *On Tithes*, i. pp. 131-136.

on in presence of a justiciar of the King; but the general ecclesiastical jurisdiction of Rome seems undisturbed.

In 1406, in the first parliament of James I., 'to the honour of God and halie Kirk, it is statute and ordained, that the halie Kirke joyis and bruke, and the ministers of it, their aulde privileges and freedomes; and that no man let (hinder) them to set their landes and teindes, under the paine that may follow be spiritual law or temporal.' This, however, is not a law establishing tithes and the application of them when paid, like that of Edgar in England, but a general confirmation of the Church's rights, with a special authority to do what we shall hereafter see was the cause of much of the difficulty attending the subject, *i.e.* to set or let out the right to draw teinds.

The ecclesiastical organisation of Scotland prior to the Reformation was something like this:—There were thirteen bishoprics. The Archbishop of *St. Andrews*, whose chapter arose out of a Culdee settlement, had eight suffragans: *Dunkeld*, of which the original chapter was Culdaic; *Aberdeen*, *Moray*, *Brechin*, also originally Culdaic; *Dunblane*, the only bishopric founded by a subject; *Ross*, *Caithness*, and *the Orkney Islands*—originally a Norwegian diocese and under the episcopal superintendence of the Archbishops of Drontheim till the reign of James III. The Archbishop of *Glasgow*, whose see was (as a bishopric) of almost mythical antiquity, had three suffragans: *Galloway*, a very ancient bishopric arising from the Church of St. Ninian; *Argyle*, at one time part of the see of Dunkeld (which retained Iona at the time of the foundation of the Argyle bishopric); and *the Isles*, which arose out of the old bishopric of Man and the Western Isles—a see under that of Drontheim—but which ultimately took shape as bishopric of the Hebrides, including Bute and Arran, with the bishop's seat at Iona, which had passed away from Dunkeld.

The chapters of St. Andrews, Dunblane, Galloway, and the Isles were at one period or another composed of regulars, but other bishoprics probably had similar chapters. Generally the chapter of each cathedral consisted of certain secular or parochial clergymen holding benefices within the diocese, canons deriving their title from their prebenda or living, and other clerics who held office in the cathedral. The churches of the diocese whose fruits, tithes, lands, or gifts were appropriated to the maintenance of the bishop were styled *mensal* churches;[1] those whose fruits went to the support of the prebendaries, *common* churches. When a parish minister, as sometimes, though infrequently, happened, drew his whole tithes himself, he was called *persona ecclesiæ*. A priest whose right came through the chapter was called in England *parson imparsonee*; he drew the rectorial or great tithes, and the lesser tithes were drawn by his vicar, who served the cure of the parish, with the title of *vicarius pensionarius*.

The revenues of a bishopric were derived from the lands held by the see, and known as the *temporality*; and from tithes and ecclesiastical dues, which were termed the *spirituality*. It was only a share of the spirituality which fell to the minister who served the cure, and perhaps the following table will illustrate more clearly the different rights of parties :—

A cathedral, or monastery, drew all temporalities.

A cathedral, *or* monastery, *or* rector, drew all the *decimæ bladi* or great tithes (*or* the rector received a share, while the cathedral or monastery drew the rest).

The vicar drew the *decimæ fœni*, or small tithes, and personal offerings—subject, however, to arrangement with the cathedral, *or* monastery, *or* rector, if it was thought the vicar was getting too much.

In addition to the cathedrals, there grew up collections of secular clergy in what were known as collegiate churches, which were never richly endowed, and which only maintained their

---

[1] The Bishops of Argyle had no mensal churches, and instead received the teinds of particular lands in each parish. This was known as the *bishop's quarter.*—Elliot, *Teind Court Procedure*, p. 34.

prebendaries and collegiate churches. There were thirty-eight such colleges; the last founded before the Reformation was that of Biggar, in 1545; and it received, among other gifts, the patronage of the church of Thankerton, with the rents, fruits, and emoluments, from Lord Fleming, to whom the Abbey of Kelso had surrendered its rights, and the perpetual vicarage of the parish church of Dunrod in the stewartry of Kirkcudbright from the Abbey of Holyrood. Of such miscellaneous endowments were the riches of cathedrals, of monasteries, and of collegiate churches alike composed. Sometimes a kind of tithe called *can* and *conveth* is referred to. *Can* subsists in the word *cain* or *kain* fowl, *i.e.* a reek hen, or hen payable from every house where a chimney smoked. *Conveth* seems originally to have been a due collected by a feudal lord from his vassal. Innes cites a grant by Malcolm IV. to the canons of Scone, whose church had recently been burnt, from every plough belonging to their church, 'for their *conveth* at the Feast of All Saints, a cow and two swine, and four *clamni* of meal, and ten thraves of oats, and ten hens and two hundred eggs, and ten bunches of candles, and four nummatus of soap, and twenty half malæ of cheese.'[1]

Where the churches and tithes were in the possession of a monastery, they were dealt with by the Order according to their rules and the canon law. The Abbey of Kelso was probably the richest of all such foundations. Such great institutions were of course formidable rivals to the bishoprics, and they afforded the most tempting spoil to laymen, in so far as their endowments could be received *in commendam.* Thence, as we shall see, arose the lordships of Erections, which were merely great religious lordships converted into civil lordships.

[1] *Scotch Legal Antiquities*, pp. 204-5. The lecture on 'The Old Church' gives the clearest and most comprehensive view of the Scottish Establishment prior to the Reformation with which I am acquainted, and I have made frequent use of it in this chapter.

We have no means of knowing when Scotland was generally covered with parishes, but the work was not complete in 1581, for by c. 100 of that year it is provided that 'every paroch kirk, and sameikil (so much) bounds *as shall be found to be a sufficient and competent parochin theirfoir*, shall have their awn pastor,' etc.[1]

What, then, was the position of the Church in Scotland when the Reformation burst?

We have seen that the Culdees did not exact tithes, but owned lands, possibly in family and hereditary groups; that those lands were attached to the churches or monasteries which, under the reformation carried out by David I., took the place of the Culdees' establishments; that the duty of tithe-paying was recognised under David and his immediate successors; that when lands were given to a monastery, the tithes of the lands were usually bestowed with them, but not necessarily so; that when the king gave grants to his nobles, it was usually under burden of payment of tithes; that tithes were not exigible parochially, except where the cure was served by a rector; that in the great majority of cases the tithes of parishes were drawn by monasteries, or clergy of monasteries, who gave the vicar who served the cure such sum as might be agreed upon. In Scotland, at the date of the Reformation, there were 940 parishes, and of these 262 were patronate, *i.e.* the patronage was in the hands of laymen, whose presentees, as rectors, nominally had right to the whole parochial teinds, but often by arrangement left a large portion of them in the hands of their patrons; and the remaining 678 were patrimonial, *i.e.* the patronage and teinds were in the hands of bishops or monasteries, who from the time of Alexander III. usually allotted one-third of the teinds to the vicars. The rich clergy were very rich; the parochial clergy, unless they were sons of noble families, were very poor.

[1] Connell, i. p. 210.

Prior to the Reformation the *ipsa corpora* of teinds was usually drawn, unless by usage or agreement a fixed number of bolls of victual was accepted annually in place of the teinds being actually drawn.

Perhaps, before leaving the pre-Reformation period, it may be remarked that, although parochial churches are frequently referred to in the records, too much is not to be understood by the term church. The stone churches were very few. The chancel of the church of Dollar, in Clackmannanshire, was praised in 1336, but it was constructed of hewn oak; at the same date the chancel of Edrom, in the Merse, was thatched with straw. The Reformation storm is not responsible for the destruction of our parish churches, for such as existed were, for the most part, built of unsubstantial materials, and hence easily fell into decay. It was, too, the army of Henry of England that was responsible for the ruin of Melrose, Kelso, Dryburgh, Jedburgh, Eccles, Newbattle, Holyrood, and Haddington.[1]

[1] *Quarterly Review*, vol. lxxxv., art. by Joseph Robertson, pp. 146-7.

CHAPTER IV

TITHES IN SCOTLAND DURING THE REFORMATION PERIOD AND SUBSEQUENTLY: 1560-1628

WHAT Machiavelli wrote of the ecclesiastical principalities of Italy in the beginning, may be applied to Scotland in the end, of the sixteenth century. The greatest difficulty, he says, is to get into possession, 'because they are gained either by fortune or virtue, but kept without either, being supported by ancient statutes universally received in the Christian Church, which are of such power and dignity they do keep their prince in his dignity, let his conversation or conduct be what it will.' 'These,' he continues with a cynicism which scarcely veiled the truth, 'are the only persons who have lands and do not defend them; subjects, and do not govern them; and yet their lands are not taken from them, though they never defend them; nor their subjects dissatisfied, though they never regard them; so that their principalities are the happiest and most secure in the world by being managed by a supernatural power, above the wisdom and contrivance of man' (*The Prince*, chap. xi).[1]

---

[1] As regards the 'subjects,' however, the tenants and vassals of the great abbeys of Scotland had, as Sir Walter Scott points out, 'many advantages over those of the lay barons, who were harassed by constant military duty, until they became desperate and lost all relish for the arts of peace. The vassals of the Church, on the other hand, were only liable to be called to arms on general occasions, and at other times were permitted in comparative quiet to possess their farms and feus. They, of

Before the Reformation came it had been long foreseen. The wealth of the upper clergy, whose lands covered half Scotland, brought plentiful abuses in its train, and the poverty of the vicars and of the curates contrasted strangely with the magnificence of their superiors. Too much weight must not be placed on the verses which satirically describe the clergy, because the abuses of the Church have at all times afforded material for satire; but the words put into the mouth of Duncan Laidens *alias* Makgregouris (who was beheaded 16th June 1552) are as interesting in their way as those of Piers Plowman on the same subject. Thus run three verses of his *Legacy* :—

> To my Curate, negligence I resign,
>   Therewith his parishioners for to teach;
> Another gift I leave him as condign,
>   Sloth with ignorance, seldom for to preach,
>   The souls he commits for to bleach
> In purgatory till they be washen clean,
> Pure religion thereby for to sustain.
>
> To the Vicar I leave diligence and cure
>   To take the utmost cloth and the kirk cow [1]
> More than to put the corpse in sepulture;
>   Have poor widow six grice and a sow,
>   He will have one to fill his belly fou.
> His thought is more upon the Pasch fines
> Than the souls in purgatory that pines.
>
> Coppression the Parson I leave until (unto)
>   Poor men's corn to hold upon the rig
> Till he get the teynd all whole at his will,

course, exhibited superior skill in everything that related to the cultivation of the soil, and were, therefore, both wealthier and better informed than the military retainers of the restless chiefs and nobles in their neighbourhood.'—*The Monastery*, chap. i.

[1] For burial dues, see *supra*, p. 34, for similar demands in England in lieu of hypothetically unpaid personal tithes.

Suppose the bairns their bread should go thig (beg),
His purpose is no kirks for to big:
So fair a bairn teme God has him sendin,
These seven years the choir will ly unmenden.'[1]

Those verses graphically illustrate the ordinary heritor's view of things before the Reformation. The parson who has nominal charge of the parish insists on his teinds of the crops, whoever suffers, while he fails to carry out what was then his legal obligation, to maintain the choir of the village church; his vicar is as particular about the vicarage teinds or their equivalent, which he seizes when a poor man dies; and the curate, who should preach, is too lazy to do his work. Such was the state of rural Scotland, and it was a state which, as Froude says of the Reformation in England under Wycliffe, 'begot in the mind of the people indignation at lies and injustice, and the revival of earnestness was accompanied with a furious spirit of political revolt.'

That the Church was thoroughly rotten at the time of the Reformation is sufficiently clear if we confine our attention to the statutes of her diocesan and other councils, without regard to the accusations of the Reformers. That such regulations should have been necessary speak for themselves. Thus, Archbishop Foreman (Archbishop in 1514), in a synod at St. Andrews, sanctions statutes sternly censuring clerical non-residence and concubinage, ordering that chapels which are not sufficiently endowed should be closed; that those who have the cure of souls are only to have their faculties renewed after examination; that beneficed clergy are themselves to administer the sacraments to their parishioners, and to dismiss their substitutes; and that all rectors, vicars, curates, and

---

[1] Cf. Langlands:—
> For the tithing of a duck,
> Or an apple or an aie (egg),
> They make men swere upon a boke,
> Thus they fouler Christes faie.

chaplains are to be present *in propria persona* in their churches on Sundays.[1]

A Provincial Council of Clergy at Edinburgh in 1549, presided over by Archbishop Hamilton, passed many laws to the same effect—forbidding, especially, concubinage by the clergy; the promotion of clergymen's illegitimate children to benefices; the wearing of yellow, green, and other unbecoming garments; ordering the inspection of monasteries; condemning the practice of deans receiving bribes to hush up offences; enjoining rectors of parishes to preach at least four times a year; strictly enjoining residence on all beneficed and pensioned clergy; providing for an examination of all parochial clergy on account of the known want of qualification of many, and for an income of at least £20 annually to all vicars.

In January 1552 another Provincial Council met, also in Edinburgh; and among other matters it forbade the alienation or letting on long lease of Church property, with the view of enriching the friends and relations of the clergy, and the consequent impoverishment of the successors to the benefices.

The years between 1546 (when Cardinal Beaton was murdered) and 1553 were the breathing-time of the Church, and the statutes of the two Edinburgh Councils show that the Church was desirous of putting her house in order; but it was too late. Not that those in high places always sympathised with reform, as is shown by the curious memorial submitted by Aberdeen chapter to their bishop, in which, after begging him to cause his diocesan clergy to reform their lives, and to provide for at least one sermon before the beginning of Lent, and one more between that and Easter in every parish church, they appeal to the bishop himself to show a good and edifying example, particularly by breaking off an illicit connection by which he is 'greatly slandered.'

This is indeed, as the Catholic historian of the Church says,

---

[1] Bellesheim, *Catholic Church in Scotland*, ii. pp. 119-124.

'a convincing and melancholy testimony to the decay of moral and religious discipline in the Scottish Church, and to her urgent need of reform.'[1]

A Provincial Council held in Edinburgh in 1559 enacted *inter alia* that archbishops and bishops should not collate their sons to benefices in their own churches—such collation should be *ipso facto* void and null; that prelates who marry their daughters to barons or landed gentry having less than £100 of rental should not give them portions from the patrimony of the Church[2]—an abuse satirised by Sir David Lindsay in his *Three Estates* ;[3] feuing or leasing out Church lands is prohibited; but the greater tithes, when not collected by the clergy for themselves, may be leased to farmers and labourers on the glebe at a moderate sum.[4] This was the last Provincial Council of the Church before the Reformation.

From the words of the clergy themselves we can best judge of the abuses of the day. We see the parish clergy ignorant, neglectful, with small or irregular stipends; while the higher clergy live in luxury, wear gorgeous apparel, promote their sons to benefices, and give the husbands of their daughters portions of the Church's patrimony, and feu or lease out Church lands to their own profit, while the parochial churches suffer. Such was the state of the Church in Scotland at the time of the Reformation. Any one who imagines that the country was neatly mapped out into parishes, each with its presentee drawing a comfortable stipend, and that on the bursting of the storm the lords rushed into the Church's vineyard, trampling it down and leaving a waste where once had been a garden, is entirely mistaken. The appropriation of tithes and ecclesiastical lands by the laity was one of the moot

---

[1] Bellesheim, ii. p. 240.   [2] *Ibid.* p. 245.
[3] That Prelatis dochtouris of this natioun
Ar maryit with sic superfluitie,
They will nocht spair to gif twa thowsand pound
With their dochtouris to ane nobill man.
[4] Bellesheim, ii. pp. 249-50.

flagrant scandals of the Reformation; but the Church had familiarised the nobles to the idea of holding benefices on the easiest terms. James, Duke of Ross, brother to King James IV., was only twenty-one when he was made Archbishop of St. Andrews. He died in 1503, and the see was kept vacant for six years until Alexander Stuart, a natural son of King James IV., was twenty-two; shortly afterwards Pope Julius II. conferred on him the Abbey of Dumfermline and priory of Coldingham *in commendam*. The ecclesiastical position of such a prince was nominal: he died fighting by his father's side at Flodden. James V. is said to have threatened the bishops of his time that unless they reformed their lives he would send some of them to be dealt with by his uncle Henry VIII.; and in his last Parliament, that of 1541, he warned Churchmen that it was their disorderly lives which brought the Church into contempt.[1] Yet James's own natural children held as infants many abbeys *in commendam*. The Regent Arran's illegitimate brother, John Hamilton, became Abbot of Dunkeld; and in July 1547 the Regent wrote to the Pope urging that another brother, James, should be made Archbishop of Glasgow, with a grant from the revenues of that see of £100 to still two other brothers, David and Claud. A son of the Earl of Huntly became Bishop of Aberdeen; a son of the Earl of Lennox was Bishop of Caithness when only twenty years of age. Pope Paul III., when appointing Robert Reid to be Bishop of Orkney, charged the revenues of the see with a pension of £20 to a youthful cleric of fourteen, and another of 80 marks to an illegitimate son of James V., also a cleric, who had not yet attained the maturity of eight years![2]

Although the Reformation did not take regular steps until 1560, there had of course been loud mutterings long before, almost contemporaneously with the suppression of the monasteries in England; and among the charges against John

---

[1] Bellesheim, ii. p. 161.   [2] *Ibid.* pp. 196-7.

Rough and John Knox in 1545 we find there was one that they had taught 'that tithes by God's law do not appertain necessarily to Churchmen.' Spotswood, who tells the tale, adds: 'This last article I would not omit, because it is alleged by those that penned the story. Whether it was a point of John Rough's preaching or not, I cannot say; but for John Knox, it is clear by his sermons and writings still extant that he held it a point of high sacrilege to rob and spoil the Church of tithes. It is true that many in these times, offended with the extortion of Churchmen, did hold that tithes belonged not to the Church by any divine right; and knowing that this opinion would find easie passage among the people, as also serve to abridge the means and power of Churchmen, they were the more ready to deliver such doctrines; but this was done rather out of passion than judgment.'[1]

When John Knox framed his Constitution for the Reformed Church in January 1560, he certainly did not forget the tithe and the Church property, which he appears to have fondly believed would pass from the Catholic Church to that of the Reformer. He did not suggest that every minister should receive the same stipend, for, if so, with the unequal demands 'one would suffer penury and another superfluity.' 'Therefore we judge [fifth head] that every Minister should have sufficient wherewith to keep an house, and be sustained honestly in all things necessary, forth of the Rents of the Church which he serveth, conform to his quality and the necessity of time: wherein it is thought that every Minister shall have forty bolls meal, and twenty bolls malt, with mony to buy other provision to his house, and serve his other necessities; the modification whereof is to be referred to the judgment of the Church; which shall be made every year at the chusing of the Elders and Deacons; providing always, that there be advanced to every Minister provision for a quarter of a year beforehand of all things.'[2]

[1] Spotswood, *History*, p. 86.   [2] *Ibid.* p. 157.

There is no ambiguity about the sixth head, 'Of the Rents and Patrimony of the Church,' which may be cited in full :—

The Sixth Head, of the Rents and Patrimony of the Church.

' Two sorts of men; that is, the Preachers of the Word and the Poor, besides the Schools, must be sustained upon the rents of the Church ; wherefore it would be considered how and of what the same is to be raised. For to our grief we hear that some Gentlemen are now more rigorous in exacting the Tithes and other duties, paid before to the Church, than ever the Papists were, and so the tyranny of Priests is turned into the tyranny of Lords and Lairds. For this we require, that the Gentlemen, Barons, Lords, Earls, and others be content to live upon their own Rents, and suffer the Church to be restored to her right and liberty, that by her restitution the poor that heretofore have been oppressed may now receive some comfort and relaxation.

' It is a thing most reasonable that every man have the use of his own Tithes, providing that he answer the Deacons and Treasurer of the Church of that which shall be reasonably appointed unto him, and that the uppermost cloth, the Corpresent, the Clerkmail, the Pasche-offerings, Tith-ale, and other the like exactions be discharged for ever. And because not only the Ministers, but also the Poor and Schools must be sustained upon the Tithes, we think it more expedient, that Deacons and common Treasurers of the Church be appointed to receive the whole Rents appertaining thereto, than the Ministers themselves, and that commandment may be given that no man either receive or intromit with anything belonging to the sustentation of the foresaid persons, but such as shall be appointed thereto by the Church.

' If any shall think this prejudicial to those that profess the Tithes by virtue of leases, we would have them know that unjust possession is no possession before God ; and that those of whom they acquired their right were thieves and murtherers, and had no power to alienate the Patrimony and common good of the Church: yet do we wish recompence to be made to such as have debursed sums of money to these unjust possessors, so that the same had not been given of late in prejudice of the Church, or no collusion used. For which purpose we think it expedient, that whosoever have the tithes of any Church in part or whole, be warned to produce his right, that, cognition being taken thereof, a reasonable recompence may be given them, before the years that are to run, the profits of years past deduced and considered, so that the Church in end may receive her liberty and freedom.

'The Tithes that we think must be lifted for the use of the Church, are the Tithes of Hay, Hemp, Lint, Cheese, Fish, Calf, Veal, Lamb, Wool, and all sorts of Corn. But because these will not suffice to discharge the necessaries of the Church, we think that all things dotate to hospitality in times past, with all annual rents both to Burgh and Land, pertaining to Priests, Chanteries, Colleges, Chaplanries, and Friers of all orders, to the sisters of the Seynes, and all other of that sort, be retained to the use of the Church or Churches within the Towns or Parishes where they were founded: likewise the whole revenues of the Temporalities of Bishops, Deans, and Archdeacons; with all rents of lands pertaining to Cathedral Churches, which must be applied to the entertainment of Superintendents and Universities. And farther, we think that Merchants and Craftsmen in free Burghs, who have nothing to do with manuring the ground, ought to make some provision in their cities and towns and dwelling-places for the support of the Church, and necessities thereof.

'The Ministers, and failing of them the Readers, must be restored to their Manses and Gleibs, without which they cannot serve nor attend their Flocks; and where any Gleib exceedeth six acres of land, that which is more shall remain with the possessor till farther order be taken.'[1]

[1] Spotswood, pp. 164, 165.

'Whence he took that device of annual Deacons for collecting and dispensing the Church-rents,' says Spotswood, 'I cannot say. A Noble man being ask'd his judgment thereof, answered that it was a devout imagination, wherewith John Knox did greatly offend; yet was it no better than a dream, for it could never have taken effect. The Churchmen that went before had been provident enough in these matters, and good it had been for these that succeeded to have kept fast that which they found established to their hand, as the Archbishop of S. Andrews did at the same time advise them. For he imploying John Brand, a Monk of Halyrudhouse (who served many years after Minister at the Canongate), to go unto John Knox, willed him to say from him, that albeit he had innovated many things, and made Reformation of the Doctrine of the Church, whereof he could not deny but there was some reason; yet he should do wisely to retain the old Policy which had been the work of many Ages, or then put a better in place thereof, before he did shake the other. "Our Highland-men," he said, "have a custome, when they will break young Colts, to fasten them by the head with strong tethers, one of which they keep ever fast till the beast be thoroughly made. The multitude, that Beast with many heads, would just be so dealt with. Master Knox, I know, esteemeth me an enemy; but tell him from me he shall find it true that I speak."'[1]

The archbishop was right. Although many nobles signed the Book of Policy, it was with a significant addendum, 'That the Bishops, Abbots, Priors, and other beneficed men who had joyned themselves to the Religion should enjoy the Rents of their Benefices during their lives, they sustaining the Ministers for their parts, as was prescribed in the said Book.'

This was as devout an imagination as Knox's; while the ink was drying on the signatures, the Church was as rapidly as possible getting rid of her possessions to Churchmen's

---

[1] Spotswood, p. 174. See also Carlyle, *Heroes and Hero-Worship*—'Knox.'

friends and kinsmen, and of the very signatories the great majority, getting into their hands such possessions, forgot their adhesion to Knox's device for collecting Church rents, and kept a firm hold of what they got, thus turning, as the historian of the time says, 'greater enemies in that point of Church Patrimony than were the Papists or any other whatsoever.'[1] The Confession of Faith was adopted by the Assembly of the Estates at Edinburgh in August 1660, and here the formal history of the Reformation may be said to begin. There were, however, many of the Romish clergy attending the Assembly who voted for the adoption of the Confession, and it was long after this ere the Catholic Church could be said to be disestablished, or her clergy to be disendowed.

In 1661 the Crown, however, took a share in the work of annexing the benefices of the weakened Church. The revenues of the Crown were found insufficient to maintain the Court of Queen Mary, who had now returned from France; and as an easy way of raising funds the prelates of the weakened Church were called before the Council and asked to make a suitable contribution from their benefices. As it was only by the Queen's favour that the prelates could hope for any revenue at all, looking at the Reformers' attitude, they were scarcely in a position to refuse, and with great reluctance agreed to allow the Queen to appoint collectors to gather one-third of their whole revenues, to be disposed of at the Queen's pleasure, the prelates on the other hand being secured in the remaining two-thirds.

The Assembly of 1564 presented a petition to the Queen that some provisions should be made for the ministers, 'and their livings assigned them in the places where they served, or at least in the parts next adjacent;' that benefices which had become vacant since March 1558 should be filled; 'that no Bishoprick, Abbacy, Priory, Deanry, Provostry, or other Benefice having more churches than one annexed thereto,

[1] Spotswood, p. 175.

should be disponed in time coming to any one man, but that the churches thereof being dissolved, the same should be provided to several persons, so as every man having charge may serve at his own church according to his vocation;' and as to teinds, 'that some order should be divised for the relief of the poor labourers of the ground who are oppressed in their Tithes by Leases set over their heads, and they thereby forced to take unreasonable conditions.'

The Queen answered that she did not see her way to 'defraud herself of so great a part of the Patrimony of the Crown as to put Patronages of Benefices forth of her own hands, seeing the publick necessities of the Crown did require a great part of the Rents to be still retained. Notwithstanding, Her Majesty was pleased that her own necessity being supplied, after it should be considered what might be a reasonable sustentation to the Ministers, a special assignation should be made to them forth of the nearest and most commodious places, wherewith Her Majesty should not intermeddle, but suffer the same to come to their use.' As regarded the trouble caused by the exactions of those who had leased the right to tithe land, the Queen's answer is included in a general phrase that Her Highness promised to do therein as the Estates convened in Parliament should appoint.[1]

The Assembly replied that as to the Queen's offer to provide for the ministers when her own necessities were supplied, 'That good order did require Ministers first to be provided, Schools for instructing the youth maintained, the fabrick of Churches repaired and upheld, and the poor and indigent members of Christ sustained; all which ought to be furnished out of the Tithes, which are the proper Patrimony of the Church. These things done, if any thing were remaining, that Her Majesty and Council might use it as they should think expedient.'[2]

At James's baptism in 1566 the rite was celebrated by the

[1] Spotswood, pp. 190, 191.　　　[2] *Ibid.* p. 193.

Archbishop of St. Andrews and the Bishops of Dunkeld, Dunblane, and Ross and other Romish clergy, and about the same time the Crown restored to the archbishop his former jurisdiction in confirming executors, collating to benefices, etc. The General Assembly took this greatly to heart, but it does not appear that the archbishop attempted to exercise the restored functions;[1] and to meet the ministers' constant complaints the Court offered them a sum out of the teinds which were collected. By an Act of the Privy Council, therefore, in that year, all benefices not exceeding 300 merks Scots or £16, 1s. 4½d. sterling annually were assigned to such persons as the General Assembly should appoint; and by another Act a portion of the rents of such other benefices as should amount to the sum of £10,000 Scots and 400 chalders of victual were appropriated for the general support of the ministry.[2] This was 'accepted under protestation that the same should not prejudice their right to the Tithes, nor be accompted as a satisfaction for the same.' 'For these they held to be the proper Patrimony of the Church,' continues Spotswood, 'and so justly belonging thereto, as that they ought not to be paid to any others, under whatsoever colour or pretext. But this protestation availed not, only it sheweth what was the judgment of the Church in that time concerning Tithes.'[3]

The marriage of Mary and Bothwell was celebrated on 15th May 1567[4] by Adam, Bishop of Orkney, after the manner of the Reformed Church; and it was the same bishop who crowned the infant James at Stirling, when John Knox preached the sermon.[5] In the same year, among the Articles agreed to by the Assembly and the few noblemen who accepted the invitation to join with the Assembly were the following:—

'That until the perfect order might be taken for restoring

---

[1] Spotswood, p. 198. [2] Connell, i. p. 154.
[3] Spotswood, p. 199-200. [4] *Ibid.* p. 203. [5] *Ibid.* p. 211.

Patrimony of the Church, the Act of Assignation of the thirds of Benefices for the sustentation of the Ministry should be put in due execution. That in first lawful Parliament which should be kept, or sooner if occasion might serve, the Church of Christ within this kingdom should be fully restored unto the Patrimony belonging to the same. . . . It was farther agreed that in the next Parliament, or otherwise at the first occasion, order should be taken for the ease of the labourers of the ground in the payment of their Tithes, and that the same should not be disponed to any others without their advice and consent.'[1]

This was very well in theory, but a significant comment upon it is that one of the rewards given to Kirkcaldy of Grange for his pursuit of Bothwell was the gift of the Priory of Pittenweem.[2] One of the petitions to the Regent in 1568 from the Church asks 'that remedy might be provided against the chapping and changing of Benefices, diminution of rentals, and selling of Tithes in long Leases to the defrauding of ministers and their successors.'[3]

By the Act 1567, *c.* 10, the complaints of the clergy were to some extent acknowledged, for that Act narrates that 'ministers had been long defrauded of their stipends, swa (so) that they are becummin in great poverty and necessity,' and enacts that 'the haill thirds of the haill benefices of this realme sall now instantlie and in all times to cum, first be payed to the ministers . . . ay and quhill the kirk come to the full possession of their proper patrimonie quhilk is the teinds.'[4] The Assembly was authorised to appoint collectors to uplift the thirds, and immediately did so.

The thirds of the teinds were thus collected, until in 1573 the Regent Morton procured the consent of the Church to their collection by the Crown, under promises of more liberal provisions to the clergy, and that the stipend of each parish

---

[1] Spotswood, pp. 209, 210. [2] *Ibid.* p. 213.
[3] *Ibid.* p. 228. [4] Connell, i. p. 156.

should be paid out of its own teinds. The Commission of Platt was appointed to modify stipends, but its proceedings were very unsatisfactory to the ministers, whose financial position was in no way improved by the new arrangement.

Year after year they made their complaint, but little or nothing was done to help them. Worse than all, they saw the patrimony of the Church disappearing before their eyes during the king's minority. The form of bestowing benefices on laymen as commendators was abandoned, and those who had acquired 'rights' to religious houses and their endowments obtained from the king *jure coronæ* grants as Lords of Erection. Such grants were under burden of payment of the thirds, or of providing suitable stipends for ministers; but to exact those beneficial provisions was a hard and sometimes an impossible task. Many churches were left without provision, and were abandoned by the ministers. It appears that in 1596 there were about four hundred parish kirks destitute of ministers 'by and attour the kirks of Argyll and the Isles.'[1]

When in 1587 James VI. attained majority, an Act was passed (*c.* 29) to annex to the Crown the whole lands of the beneficed clergy. It proceeded on the narrative that much of the clergy's lands had been given to the Church by the Crown, and that it was necessary for the exigencies of the State, and to avoid the imposition of taxes, that all Church lands should be held in future by the Crown. It is not quite clear whether teinds were intended to be excepted from this appropriation or not, but it is almost certain that they were excluded. In 1592 a new Act to the same effect was passed, for the king had continued his ruinous habit of making Erections of Church benefices to those who were only too ready to take all they could get. It will be remembered that in 1592 the Presbyterian form of government was established by Parliament; and a commission was appointed to deal with the burning question

[1] Connell, i. p. 161.

of ministers' stipends, but nothing was done.[1] In 1596 the General Assembly proposed a plan by which every clergyman should be provided for from the teinds of his own parish, but nothing came of it.

All this time the tithes of the old Church lived on, although in altered circumstances, Presbyterians in many cases holding the nominal rank of the 'dignified clergy' of the olden time. When in 1606 James succeeded in restoring bishops who should really discharge episcopal functions as they were understood in England, he discharged their benefices of the payment of thirds to the collectors, making it obligatory upon the bishops, however, 'to maintain the ministers serving at the cure of the kirks of their saids bishopricks, upon the readiest of their said thriddes, according to the ordinar assignations made, or reasonablie to be made thereanent.'[2] This was not a satisfactory state of things, but up to 1617 the clergy had to get on as best they could upon what they could extract from the fund made up by the thirds of the tithes as collected.

When in 1617 James came back from England to visit his elder kingdom, its ecclesiastical position was somewhat extraordinary. The suppression of the Catholic Church in 1560, six years before he was born, had been confirmed by the Parliament of 1592, when he was twenty-six; yet he had been baptized by a Catholic Archbishop of St. Andrews, and his queen, though the daughter of rigid Lutherans, had been received into the Catholic Church by Father Abercromby about 1600. The period of the Reformation in Scotland is almost exactly covered by his life of fifty-nine years; that the avowed Presbyterianism of the people took so long to settle itself was largely due to his want of real dependence upon any particular form of Church government. In England he was so persuaded of the appropriateness of the kind of episcopacy of which he approved, that it is not at all surprising that he

[1] Connell, i. p. 177.   [2] *Ibid.* i. p. 178.

should have thought fit to remodel the Scottish Church on similar lines; but that he can have imagined that by taking in hand the virtually civil offices of the Scottish bishops which still existed, and having the holders of them consecrated by English bishops, he had succeeded, seems to show an extraordinary confusion of ideas. As Father Bellesheim observes, the so-called Scottish prelates being in the eyes of the Roman and the English Church simply laymen, 'the result of this singular proceeding, of course, was that whereas Anglicanism recognises as essential the three orders of bishop, priest, and deacon, the unfortunate Church of Scotland had to content herself with the episcopate alone.' In other words, when James came to Scotland in 1617 the country was covered by Presbyterian parishes, and yet possessed certain nondescript bishops who were not Romish, nor Anglican, nor Presbyterian. James brought with him to admire his work the Bishop of Ely, and Laud, the future archbishop, and it is to be hoped they understood it.[1]

It was to the Scottish Church of this anomalous kind that the great benefits of a reform of the law of teinds was conferred, Parliament in 1617 appointing a Commission, which numbered eight prelates, with power, 'out of the teinds of every parochin to appoint and assigne at their discretions, ane perpetual local stipend to the ministers present and to come.' It is really from this date that the maxim *decimæ debentur parocho*—the tithes belong to the parish—can be said to be recognised in Scotland. Theoretically it had been admitted for centuries, but as a matter of practice it had been little known during the subsistence of the Catholic Church, and was entirely ignored by the civil power from 1560. The clergy, now, were no longer to receive certain stipends out of a general fund formed of such Thirds as could be collected

---

[1] As to the 'Tulchan' bishops see Carlyle's *Oliver Cromwell*, 1871 ed., i. p. 36. Laud found in Scotland 'no religion at all.'—Wharton's *Laud* (1695), cited by Carlyle, *ibid.* p. 37.

and were not otherwise required, but were definitely to obtain from the tithes of their own parishes such sums as might be fixed by the Commission. The minimum stipend was fixed at five chalders (16 bolls=1 chalder) of victual, *i.e.* corn or meal, or 500 merks, £27, 15s. 6⅓d. sterling, 'or proportionally part of victual and part thereof in money, according as the fruits and rents of the Kirk may yield and afford, and as the said Commissioners shall think expedient.'[1] The Commissioners were not to meddle with any stipends that were already above the minimum. The maximum stipend was fixed at eight chalders of victual, or 800 merks, £44, 9s. sterling.

This Commission was very welcome to the clergy, but its powers expired at Lammas 1618. A new Commission was appointed in 1621, but it seems never to have acted. James died in 1625, and the record of his work for the Church of Scotland is meagre and confusing enough.

Meantime, it has to be observed that the disastrous practice of leasing out tithes went on quite as commonly in the early days of the Reformation as in the latter days of Catholicism, and by ministers who happened to be in right of their teinds as titulars just as openly as by the bishops. The practice was strictly prohibited by Acts 1581, *c.* 101, and 1585, *c.* 11. Tacks were, however, conditionally recognised by Acts 1594, *c.* 203; 1617, *c.* 4; 1621, *c.* 15.

Several curious instances of such tacks are given by Connell,[2] as in the cases of the parishes of Glassary, Auchterarder, Birse, etc., secured in the remaining two-thirds for life, and relieved of the maintenance of any of the ministers of the Reformed Church.[3]

An interesting glimpse of the fortunes of a post-Reformation parsonage and its teinds is given in the case of *Duff* v. *The Earl of Seafield*, Nov. 9, 1883, 11 R. 126.

The parish of Keith, in the bishopric of Moray, fell into the

---

[1] Connell, i. pp. 184-5. [2] *Ibid.* i. p. 190.
[3] Spotswood, p. 183.

hands of James VI. on the death of the Bishop of Moray, and was erected into a parsonage by the king in 1590, confirmed by a special Act of Parliament in 1592. In 1601 the minister of Keith granted a tack of the teinds to Lord Saltoun for nineteen years for a teind duty of 500 merks for parsonage teinds and £10 for vicarage. In 1609 an Act of Parliament was passed containing a ratification of Lord Saltoun's title, and, taking into account the great services of his family, it declared 'the tack of teinds and the rights of parsonages to be good and sufficient lawful and valid rights for bruiking of the teind sheaves and other sheaves during the lifetime and space contained in the said tacks, and for bruiking the rights of patronage in all time coming.' In 1612 Lord Saltoun assigned the tack to Lord Ochiltree. In 1618 the Commissioners appointed under the Act 1617, ch. 3, to see that churches had ministers and that ministers had stipends (it had nothing to do with the valuation of teinds), proceeded to inquire into the state of Keith. There were two churches in the parish, the parish church proper and the kirk of Grange. The Commissioners called upon those interested in the teinds of Keith to produce their titles. There appeared the Bishop of Aberdeen, who was also minister of Keith parish; and the Bishop of Moray, in whose diocese the parish was, and who appeared in name and as procurator for the minister of Grange. The two bishops declared that, although Grange was not a 'paroche kirk bot allenarlie ane pendicle of the paroche kirk of Keythe,' yet for many years it had been provided with a separate minister, and that, 'in respect of ye gritnes of ye charge of ye cure and function of ye said haill parochine of Keythe,' the arrangement should be adhered to, and a suitable stipend should be provided for the minister of Grange. Lord Ochiltree also appeared, and produced the tack to Lord Saltoun, which Lord Saltoun had conveyed to him. He renounced his right as tacksman of the vicarage benefice, and in respect of that renunciation asked a prolongation of his tack, which indeed had then but two years to run. The Commissioners, with great care, then divided the parish and apportioned the stipend, giving the minister of Keith the vicarage teinds above renounced, to the extent of 400 merks, and 700 merks of parsonage teinds, while to the minister of Grange they gave vicarage teinds to the amount of 300 merks, and 300 merks from the parsonage teinds. So far Lord Ochiltree had fared badly. He had renounced his vicarage teinds, and had been made liable in parsonage teinds to the amount of 1000 merks, whereas his rent for the tack of the whole teinds, parsonage and vicarage, was only 500 merks. However, the bargain was no one-sided one, for Lord Ochiltree received a very liberal prolongation of his tack from the date it would expire, *i.e.* 1620, for ten terms of nineteen years, bringing it down to 1810.

In 1646 Lord Ochiltree granted a sub-tack of the teinds to Gordon of Park.

Two years later Gordon of Park found himself in this position :—he was tacksman of the teinds of Kempcairn in Kilsyth and proprietor of the lands of Park, paying teind for a portion of those lands called Ordiquhill to Ogilvie of Kempcairn, while Ogilvie of Kempcairn had no right to the teinds of his lands of Kempcairn, which Gordon drew, but drew the teinds of Gordon's lands of Ordiquhill in the Park estate. So the two proprietors by contract of excambion exchanged their teind-rights, so that each should draw the teinds of his own lands.[1] It is a curious and instructive case.

In October 1625 King Charles I. endeavoured to save as much as possible for the Crown, and issued a general revocation of James I.'s grants of vacant Church benefices and of *brevi manu* usurpations after the Reformation, and in 1626 followed this by an action of reduction of all grants and claims inconsistent with the Act of Annexation of 1587. The king's

---

[1] The teinds of Ordiquhill had been acquired on tack, likewise, from the parson of Fordyce in 1604 for a period of thirty years; the tack was ultimately prorogated for a period of 203 years.

procedure caused great alarm, and in November 1626 a petition was presented to the king by the nobles, which sets forth that many of them or their predecessors, for 'faithful and memorable service' when the Crown 'was endangered by the joyned counsallis, forces, and fraud of Popische potentats and rebellious subjects, tending to subversioun of religioune and State,' had received grants of lands, teinds, etc., some of which were granted by, and others ratified in, Parliament; that the petitioners are 'not without causs affrighted at the large extent of your Majesties revocationes;' that they have no fear of their title, but beg the king to cause the actions of reduction to be stopped, and either to hold a Parliament, or to appoint 'ane competent nomber of best experienced counsellours, prelates, judges, and lawiers and pairties interest in the bissines, to conveene and treate of all that may concern your Maiestie profeite and patrimonie, and your subjectis lawfull sureties.'

To this the king, whose main object seems to have been to receive a sufficient personal grant on tolerably easy terms from those who enjoyed the Scottish benefices, agreed, and in January 1627 appointed a Commission—probably at the time intended solely in the interests of the Crown, and to force on the general submission of the doubtful rights which the king had threatened to challenge, of which the lordships of erections and other teind-rights were among the most important. He directed the Commissioners to treat with such persons as might be willing to treat as to erections and temporalities of benefices, feu-duties, 'or uthir certaine rents of silvir or victual of the said temporalities, teynds, and patronages of the said benefices;' as to what should be given them for their 'pretended rights,' or for their holding on terms of new arranged with the Crown; as to the establishment of 'a certain patrimonie to the Crowne, therewith to remain in all time coming,' the endowing of ministers, dividing parishes, and establishing manses. The Commissioners found the information before them very insufficient to enable them to deal with so large a subject, and they issued a proclamation to the presbyteries directing them to institute an inquiry into the state and worth of the teinds in each parish within its bounds—a proceeding which caused much alarm to the holders of the rights of titularity of teinds, whose oppressive action had been long resented by both ministers and heritors. 'This proclamation,' said Lord Justice-Clerk Hope in *Dunlop, etc.* v. *Commissioners of Woods and Forests*, June 2, 1858, 20 D. p. 1032, in a case in which the original papers were reprinted, and from which this account of King Charles's inquiry is largely drawn, 'was very rapidly and extensively acted upon in most parts of Scotland, with a celerity quite remarkable in those days, but accounted for by the deep interest which the parties to whom the inquiry was committed had personally in the matter. No instance is known in those days, and with the then difficulty of communication, in which the same rapidity of action took place.'

But the Commissioners had no authority to compel those with whom they were empowered to treat to agree to their terms, and they stopped short in the end of June 1627, referring the whole matter back to the king, their only decision being that the king ought to receive a constant rent and duty paid out of the whole teinds of the kingdom. The appointment of the Commissioners had its uses, however, for their inquiries frightened many titulars into voluntary submission to the Commissioners.

Matters took a new turn by the submission of the various questions which had been raised as to teinds—by (1) lords of erection, titulars and heritors; (2) bishops and clergy; (3) burghs enjoying grants for pious uses (ministers, schools, colleges, and hospitals); and (4) tacksmen of the teinds—to the Crown for decision; the king accepted the submission, and appointed in September 1628 the Commissioners of 1627 to proceed with the Commission with new and additional powers. The general scheme of the inquiry and submission was (1) to prevent the teinds being drawn in kind from the heritors; (2) to enable those liable in payment of teinds to purchase them at a fixed price; (3) to allot competent stipends to parochial clergy, and to relieve the holders of teinds from any claims at their instance, or of the patrons directly against the teinds; (4) to arrange a plan for a valuation of each heritor's teinds, which was intended to be universal over the kingdom, and to secure a fixed revenue to the king out of the teinds which would yield larger funds than the Church was supposed to require—a royal tax, also, which might fittingly be paid by those who were confirmed in rights which, more or less, were of questionable character. (Lord Justice-Clerk Hope, *ut supra*.)

The Commissioners were authorised to appoint sub-commissioners for valuation purposes, and in practice sub-commissioners were directed generally to presbyteries.

The decrees of the king following upon the submission may be briefly summarised:—

As regards teinds held by (1) lords of erection, titulars, and heritors, and (2) tacksmen, the rate of teind was fixed at 'the fifth part of the constant rent[1] which each land payeth in stock and teinds where the same are valued jointly.'

When the stock and teinds were valued separately, it was for the Commissioners to make the proper valuation. From the sum they arrived at, a fifth was to be deducted for the provi-

---

[1] Mr. Elliot observes:—'One-fifth of the rent for teind. This is shown to have been a fair equivalent for the tenth of the produce when, as was usual at the time, the rent consisted of teind and third—*i.e.* the tenant paid (1) the teind and (2) a third of the remainder of the produce of his farm in name of rent. Thus the rent of a piece of ground, the product of which was 100 bolls, is computed at 10 bolls to meet the titular's claim and 30 bolls for stock to meet the landowner's claim. These together amount to 40 bolls, one-fifth of which is 8 bolls as the valued teind. By the other method the teind of 100 bolls is 10 bolls, from which deduct one-fifth for the king's ease; the valued teind duty remains 8 bolls.' *Teind Court Procedure*, p. 24, footnote 3.

sion to the Crown, which King Charles had so constantly in view, and which now went by the name of 'the King's-ease.' Nine years' purchase of the sum which remained was the price at which a heritor might purchase the teinds from a titular, or tacksman, under burden of stipend and King's-ease.

The terms upon which the bishops' teinds were to be valued need not concern us here; the arrangement with those having right to them was a special one. On the final abolition of Episcopacy in 1689 they were appropriated by the Crown, and cannot be purchased except upon special terms.

Teinds held by burghs were to be estimated on similar terms to those held by titulars and tacksmen.[1]

Teinds held for pious uses could not be compulsorily purchased. The decreets were ratified by Parliament in 1630; subsequent Commissions were appointed in 1629, 1663, 1641, 1644, 1647, 1649. From 1649 to 1660, during the Commonwealth, Commissioners were appointed who were called 'Commissioners for visiting universities and appointing maintenance for ministers.' From 1660 to 1700 the business of valuation was not so vigorously proceeded with; the Commission was renewed in 1693. Shortly after the Union the business of the former Parliamentary Commissioners was transferred to the judges of the Court of Session, as Commissioners for Plantation of Kirks and Valuation of Teinds.

---

[1] To avoid details unnecessary to the study of the general development of the law of tithes, town stipends and burgh teinds are not dealt with here. See *Teind Court Procedure*, pp. 15, 23, 25.

CHAPTER V

TEINDS IN THE PRESENT DAY

WE have now traced the gradual development of the law of tithes. Originally an ecclesiastical duty alone, the payment of tithes was recognised as a civil obligation under Charlemagne, and the laws he made were adopted in England. Both on the Continent and in England the Church derived great benefit from the sanction given by the State to the collection of a portion of the year's produce as a contribution to the maintenance of the clergy. With the development of the pretensions of the Papacy, the Church, however, ceased to depend upon civil rulers for the observance of the duty; and when tithes were introduced into Scotland it was at a stage when the Church felt strong enough to require their payment as a thing recognised by the universal custom of Christendom. The Church law which Queen Margaret and her son David I. introduced into the Scotland of their day was that of Edward the Confessor; and it was necessary to its adoption here that it should be acknowledged, not primarily as an English observance, but as one which the whole world owned as binding upon it. There was nothing illegal in the Culdaic system; it was irregular according to the rules which were held binding in England, but it was ancient, it was associated intimately with the fortunes of powerful families, and it was familiar to the people. The innovations from the south could not well have been forced upon the nation—such as it was; the part David played was that of the reformer only.

He remodelled existing institutions in so thorough a manner upon an Anglican model that the change he accomplished well deserves to be known as the First Reformation; but he did so purely as an ecclesiastical statesman who was a true son of the Church, not as a law-giver. The Culdaic tribal system, excellent in many things, had many defects—some of them almost incident to clan government; and David may well have thought that by his work in restricting the existing institutions, and in introducing not only the regular government of dioceses but the monastic orders in their second Anglican form, he was doing much not only to forward religion—an object always very dear to him, but to settle the country. Every gift of land to bishop or monastery meant so much the more territory safe from occupation by the territorial subject-lords, who were always the chief dangers of a Scottish king. It was a great protection to such a sovereign, both as ecclesiastical reformer and politician, to work out his remedial measures for Church and State, not under any law of his own devising, but with the sanction of laws which knew no national limits, and which were accepted as obligatory by all who looked to Rome as the seat of Christ's Vicegerent. On the other hand, the Anglican Church as introduced into Scotland was distinctly an intruder, and willingly welcomed the protection of the king, as Leo had welcomed Charlemagne or John XII. had welcomed Otto, and acknowledged his authority as readily as it owned his piety.

Under David's successors, until the Wars of the Succession, things went well enough, although the Crown for one system of tribal churches had for the most part only substituted another. Nothing is so permanent as a corporation; and while a family might rise to great power in one of its sons, and sink with another, most of the monasteries went steadily on in prosperity. During the wars of Wallace and Bruce, and the long minorities of the Stuarts, this was very evident; and when James V. died the Church had for long been independent of civil authority, and lived under a law of her own, too strong to need aid from the uncertain and brief power of any king. Power and wealth brought their own abuses, and during the long and troublous times of the Second Reformation the Church and her lands and her tithes fell a prey to the civil power she had generally, though not consistently, ignored.

The Church of the Reformers had no David at its head. There was no bold reconstruction of the old Church on new lines save in Knox's brain. The Culdees had been reorganised; the Church of Beaton was simply submerged; and all the Reformers saved was from the wreckage that floated on the surface of a turbulent river.

That in the long-run the tithes, or a portion of them, were saved to the Church on a business plan does not seem to have been in any way due to Charles I.'s desire to assist the Church. His motive in carrying out the systematic valuations of teinds was to secure a provision to himself by the tax or burden called King's-annuity, and was as unconcealed as was his grandmother's bold demand to the prelates of her day to surrender one-third of their benefices for her privy purse. The history of the King's-annuity may be told in a few words. It was fixed in 1627. Charles subsequently assigned it to James Livingstone, Groom of his Bedchamber, in security of a debt of £10,000. It came by-and-by into the hands of the Earl of Loudoun, and in 1674 it was stopped by royal warrant.[1] It is still allowed as a deduction from the price of teinds in actions of valuation and sale, but it is purely fictitious.

Out of Charles's selfish legislation came much good both to the Church which collected and the heritors who paid teinds. The clergy were secured in payment of stipends by those being localled, or fixed upon the teinds of the localities where they served their cures; and the heritors were afforded a ready way, if they pleased, of ridding themselves of the payment of teinds, otherwise than to ministers with such localled stipends,

[1] See Stair's *Institutions*, bk. ii. tit. viii. 13.

by purchasing their teinds after valuation at fixed rates. Thus the tithes once again came under the direct recognition of the civil authority of the sovereign, as in the days of Charlemagne and of Edgar.

At the present day all lands in Scotland are liable in payment of teind except (1) glebes (even though feued), (2) lands held by heritors with titles which bear to be *decimis inclusis*, (3) lands of which the heritors have purchased the teinds (except as regards existing stipends), and (4) Crown lands— but Crown lands, if sold to subjects, become liable for teinds, and teind-paying lands continue to be liable for teinds when purchased by the Crown.

All teinds in Scotland belong (1) to the Crown, which draws the bishops' teinds, *or* (2) to burghs for pious uses, *or* (3) to universities, *or* (4) to titulars, *or* (5) to tacksmen, *or* (6) to patrons, *or* (7) to the proprietors of lands who have purchased their teinds or who hold their lands under titles *cum decimis inclusis*, *or* (8) to parish clergymen to whom they have been surrendered, and who hold them, as they hold their manses, for life.

All teinds may be valued by the Commissioners of Teinds on the application of (1) the heritor liable in payment, *or* (2) the person entitled to receive the teind, *or* (3) the minister of the parish in which the teind-bearing land is situated.

Bishops' teinds, teinds held by burghs for pious purposes, or by universities, cannot be compulsorily purchased. Teinds in the possession of (1) titulars or tacksmen may be bought at nine years' purchase, and (2) teinds in the possession of patrons at six years' purchase, in each case allowance being made in the purchasing heritor's favour for King's-annuity. Bishops' teinds (3) are sold by the Crown at such price as the Commissioners of Woods and Forests may fix, from eighteen to eleven years' purchase.[1]

The right of patrons as titulars of teinds has been acquired

[1] Or less. The price depends on the probabilities of allocation.

in a curious way. After the Reformation, the patron of a parish, who had at that time no right to teinds, was entitled (and specially by the Act 1612, *c.* 1) to make arrangements with the minister as to how much of the teinds the minister should draw, he taking the rest. In Acts of 1649, 1662, and 1690, relative to patronage, the patron's right to such teinds as are otherwise owned is, subject to the minister's stipend, expressly recognised. This right is *qua* patron, and was given as a compensation in 1649, when patronage was abolished; patronage was restored, but the patron kept the titularity of teinds he had acquired, and he keeps it still. This is one of the singular anomalies of the law of teinds.

Much of the difficulty which undoubtedly attends this branch of law has been due to popular confusion of *teind* and *stipend*. It is quite common to hear it said, in answer to an inquiry as to what teind means, that teinds are the contributions of the land-owning classes to the upkeep of the Church of Scotland. However true this once may have been, it is not true now; for whether the Church existed or did not exist, teinds would continue to be paid, and stipend is rather an inseparable burden on teinds than teind an equivalent term for stipend, which it has never been since the Reformation, and seldom was before that time.

The law may be more clearly stated thus:—Teinds are a property which, with certain exceptions, may be sold like feu-duties, but, unlike other property, are subject to the chance, at intervals of not less than twenty years, of the amount receivable by those owning them being affected by the Court of Teinds allowing the minister of the parish an increase or augmentation of his stipend from such teinds.

Teinds are not a *burden* on lands. As Lord President Inglis said in *Duff* v. *The Earl of Seafield*, Nov. 9, 1883, 11 R., at p. 141: 'Some confusion in argument is always introduced by looking upon teinds as a burden upon lands. Teinds are not a burden upon lands. They are a separate estate;

although, it may be added, a separate estate liable to diminution, contingent on certain circumstances of a nature more or less essentially periodic.' Stair gives his definition as follows: as 'of a burden *affecting* lands, and the profits thereof, and *being also a distinct right from the lands.*'[1]

The stipend is an inherent burden on the teinds. Lord Robertson, in the case of Prestonkirk, observed :—'The rule *decimæ debentur parochæ* never took place with us in its full extent; but all our lawyers lay it down that teinds, in whatever hands they may be, or under whatever title they may be possessed, are never held as absolute property, but are at all times subject to the burden of a suitable provision to the minister. This burden *inhæret ossibus*, and is in the eye of law perfectly inseparable from the teinds. This I consider as a fundamental proposition in the law of teinds. It is laid down as such by all our lawyers. It is a proposition which is universally true, and which admits of no exception nor no limitation whatever.'

The position of matters can best be understood by taking the case of a minister who wishes to have his stipend augmented. The procedure he must take is as follows:—He must first ascertain that twenty years have elapsed from the year when the last augmentation was granted. He then has a Summons prepared in an action of augmentation, modification, and locality against the heritors of the parish, the titulars or tacksmen of the teinds, and all others having or pretending to have an interest in the teinds of the parish, and the moderator and clerk of the presbytery in which the parish is included; and in this Summons is set forth all the circumstances which the minister thinks are likely to induce the Court to grant a suitable augmentation. He lodges a note of the stipend he then is drawing, mentioning how much is paid in money and how much in victual, what species of victual and the mode of measurement, and amount received

---

[1] *Institutions*, bk. ii. tit. viii.

by him for Communion elements, and also a rental of the parish, showing each heritor's rental. The accuracy of this rental may be admitted or it may not. If it is not questioned, or when it has been adjusted and the Court allow an augmentation, the amount of the stipend, including the augmentation, is next fixed—this is the Modification—and the process is remitted to the Lord Ordinary to fix the Locality or scheme under which the stipend so modified or appointed shall be paid. The heritors then elect a Common Agent, whose business it is to ascertain the amount of the free or surplus teind in the parish upon which the augmentation falls to be apportioned or localled. If a heritor has had his teinds valued, then in no case can he be called upon to pay more than the amount of that value; if he has purchased his teinds, he is liable up to the amount of the annual value as fixed at the valuation which preceded that sale, and for no more; but a heritor may purchase from the titular without a valuation, in which case the teinds will have as yet no fixed value; a titular, however, cannot be compelled to sell except at a price arrived at after a valuation. The amount of the teind so long as unvalued is taken at one-fifth of the land rent or arable value. A heritor who has purchased his valued teinds may surrender them in favour of the parish minister; by so doing, he frees himself and his lands from liability for any augmentation of stipend in future; the minister by this surrender becomes titular of these teinds. In preparing a scheme of locality the teinds to be first stated are (1) those which the minister holds in virtue of such surrender. There fall next (2) to be exhausted the teinds in the hands of the titular of the teinds, which includes the patron *qua* titular, teinds under tack being postponed to teinds to which the heritor has not even a temporary right; if those two are exhausted, the teinds (3) held by heritable title, acquired by purchase from the Crown or other titular, are liable; upon their exhaustion the bishops' teinds (4) held by the Crown are liable, but if such teinds have been sold, the purchaser falls into the third rank, that of heritable proprietors, and his teinds would be allocated upon for stipend before those which still belonged to the Crown. Assuming that all the other classes are exhausted, then (5) the teinds belonging to Colleges, and lastly (6) teinds appropriated to pious uses, including teinds granted to the Deans of the Chapel-Royal, are localled upon. Out of 880 teind-producing parishes, the teinds of 476 have been exhausted by augmentations;[1] this means that in those 476 parishes the minister's stipend can never be increased from the landowners, and, on the other hand, that under no circumstances (except by valuation of such part of the teinds as might have been exhausted when unvalued) could the landowners' burdens be reduced, because there is no surplus teind to be wiped out.

Stipends nearly always have been reckoned by computation of victual. A brief recapitulation of the provisions of post-Reformation law relative to stipends may not be out of place.

By the Act 1617 the Commissioners under the Act were authorised to modify at their discretion a local stipend to all parish ministers who had incomes below 500 merks, £27, 15s. 6$\frac{2}{3}$d., besides a manse and glebe, so as to approximately raise their stipend to £55, 11s. 1$\frac{1}{3}$d., or 1000 merks. Clergymen receiving more than 500 merks were excluded from this augmentation, but the Act applied to parishes up to its date unprovided with minister and stipend. In 1621, as we have seen, another body of similar Commissioners was appointed, but it does not seem to have acted. It had powers to increase all stipends at discretion except such as had been fixed by the Commission of 1617.

Matters remained in this unsatisfactory position until King Charles's Commission of 1627, the Commissioners under

---

[1] See as to augmentation of stipend, Elliot, *Teind Court Procedure*, p. 2 (footnote), p. 67, *et seq.*; Buchanan on *Teinds*, p. 257; *Juridical Styles*, iii. p. 241.

which were 'to make sufficient provision for those churches wheirof the teynds sall be reserved, and disposed as afoirsaid, if the saids churches be not already sufficientlie provydit, and for providing their ministers with sufficient local stipends and fees.' This was ratified by the Act 1633, and the minimum of ministers' stipends fixed, generally, at eight chalders of victual or 8000 merks. Of numerous subsequent Acts it may be sufficient to say that their object was distinctly to ensure the augmentation of ministers' stipends to eight chalders of victual or three chalders victually, and money for the other five. No maximum being fixed by the Act 1633, the statutory maximum of 1617 has been held to be revoked; and in 1720 the Lords of Council and Session, who had become in 1707 the permanent Commissioners on Teinds, augmented the stipend of a clergyman to 1200 merks, although in 1650 it had been fixed at 800 merks. Augmentations still continue to be granted from time to time, provided (1) that there is a surplus or free teind in the parish, and (2) that twenty years have elapsed from the date of the final interlocutor authorising the last modification. By means of augmentation the teinds of 476 parishes out of 880 teind-producing parishes have been (1893) exhausted.[1] The mode of calculating a minister's stipend at augmentations by victual is archaic and clumsy, and causes frequent misunderstanding.

When teinds were liable to be taken or drawn in kind, the annoyance caused by the delay of a titular to come promptly to the field and remove his share of the harvest must have been a prolific cause of heart-burning, for the crop could not be stacked till it was teinded. By Act 1606 a heritor was entitled, when fifteen days had elapsed after cutting his corn, to call upon the titular to teind the corn within eight days; if he failed to do so, the heritors might 'teynd and stack the same themselves.' By Act 1612, c. 5, the fifteen days of waiting were reduced to eight. Five years later the titular's

[1] Elliot, p. 2, note 3.

days of grace were limited to four days after the expiry of the eight days, but the heritor was obliged to protect from cattle the corn he teinded for the backward titular for eight days on the field.[1]

But the custom of compounding for teinding in kind was not unusual. The heritor and the titular agreed that so many bolls, hence called rental bolls, should represent the teinds, and this much simplified tithe-paying wherever an agreement was come to. After the valuations introduced in Charles I.'s reign, teinding in kind fell into desuetude; but Mr. Elliot mentions that, strangely enough, one small piece of land he knows of has been teinded in recent years.[2] This is an unexpected glimpse in the end of the nineteenth century of what, even four hundred years ago, was felt to be an anachronism.

The value of the victual in which a parish minister's stipend is usually, or in great measure, calculated is ascertained by the fiars prices, which are struck every year by the sheriff of each county. Take it that the minister's stipend is fixed at 'such a quantity of victual, half meal, half barley, in imperial weight and measure, as shall be equal to twenty chalders of the late standard weight and measure of Scotland, payable in money according to the highest fiars[3] prices of the county annually, and that for stipend,' with perhaps £10 'for furnishing Communion elements.' This involves annually a fresh calculation of the stipend, as fiars prices vary, and then the calculated sum has to be collected from the parties liable

---

[1] Connell, i. pp. 204-5.   [2] Elliot, p. 10.

[3] 'Fiars are the prices of grain in the different counties, fixed by the sheriffs respectively in the month of February, with the assistance of juries. The form of striking the fiars is prescribed by Acts of Sederunt of 21 Dec. 1723 and 29 Feb. 1728. A jury must be called, and evidence laid before them of the prices of the different grains raised in the county; and the prices fixed by the jury, and sanctioned by the judge, are termed the fiars of that year in which they are struck, and regulate the prices of all grain stipulated to be sold at the fiars prices.'—Bell's *Dictionary of the Law of Scotland*, ed. by Geo. Watson, 1890, p. 458.

in payment of teinds in such proportions as their teinds have been allocated upon in the minister's action of augmentation, modification, and locality when his stipend is fixed. It does not fall within the plan of this sketch of the historical law of tithes to discuss stipends or the calculations upon which they are arrived at in detail;[1] but it may be allowed the writer to observe that he entirely concurs in the view of the Clerk of the Court of Teinds, that future augmentations of stipend should be awarded in sterling money and not in victual, and that some means should be arrived at for converting permanently the present victual stipends into sterling money, perhaps on an estimate based on the average stipend as fixed or deduced from fiars prices for seven years previous to such conversion. Nothing can be said in defence of the present system.

The income of the clergy has, in many cases, been greatly increased by the feuing of glebes under the provisions of the Glebe Lands (Scotland) Act, 1866, but such feuing is not overlooked when an augmentation is applied for. Additions to stipends from funds provided by Parliament under the Act 50 Geo. III. *c.* 84, or other Acts, or the stipends of ministers of *quoad sacra* parishes, do not fall under our consideration, as they are virtually independent of teinds; but it may be noted that by 7 and 8 Vict. *c.* 44 the stipend of ministers of *quoad sacra* parishes is not to be less than £100 a year, or seven chalders of oatmeal, where there is a manse, or £120 a year, or eight and a quarter chalders, where there is no manse.

A clergyman of a landward parish is at present entitled to the following endowments, or privileges :—

(1) He receives out of the teinds of the parish such stipend as the Court of Teinds has localled on the parish teinds. A minister's right to the temporalities of his benefice, viz., the manse, glebe, and minister's grass, emerges with his admission to the benefice; his right to the spirituality—the stipend —is subject to the claims of a deceasing minister's next-of-kin.

[1] See Elliot, *Teind Papers*, pp. 25, *et seq.*

The term 'induction' is frequently used to describe the entrance of a minister upon his cure, but the recent decision of the First Division of the Court of Session in *Hastie v. Murtrie, supra*, puts the matter in a clear light. 'Induction,' observed the Lord President, ' is not a *nomen juris*, neither is it a *vox signata*, in the existing ecclesiastical law of Scotland. By the canon law, which was the ecclesiastical law of Scotland prior to the Reformation, induction was the legal name of a ceremony by which, after collation by the bishop of the diocese, some inferior ecclesiastical person gave the presentee actual and corporal possession of the church and benefice, under mandate from the bishop, by the use of certain symbols, which it is needless to enumerate. The ceremony was formal and imposing, and necessary to complete the presentee's title to the benefice. During the two comparatively short periods in the 17th century when the National Protestant Church of Scotland was governed by bishops, induction had again a fixed and technical meaning, and was the name for a somewhat similar ceremonial conducted under the authority of the bishop, which consisted in the inferior clergy of the diocese, after collation by the bishop, carrying the collated presentee into the church and placing him in the pulpit, or in some other conspicuous part of the church, and there delivering to him the keys of the church. But with the ceremony the name of induction as a *nomen juris* has perished. There is no use of the name in any of the numerous statutes relating to the settlement of ministers under Presbyterian Church government. In the earliest of these statutes (1567, *c.* 7) it is provided "that the examination and admission of ministers be only in the power of the Kirk." By the Act of 1592, *c.* 116, Presbyteries are "bound and astricted to receive and admit quhatsumever qualified minister presented," etc. The Act of 1690 simply revived the Act of 1592. By the Act 10 Anne, *c.* 12, restoring patronage, the Presbytery is "bound to receive and admit such qualified person or persons, minister or ministers, as shall be presented." The Aberdeen Act, 1843 (6 and 7 Vict. c. 61), bears in its title to be an Act respecting the admission of ministers, and by § 3 Presbyteries are directed to "admit and receive into the benefice." Lastly, in the Act 37 and 38 Vict. c. 82, abolishing patronage, and giving the appointment of ministers to congregations, it is enacted (§ 3) that "the courts of the Church are hereby declared to have the right to decide finally and conclusively upon the appointment, admission, and settlement in any church and parish of any person as minister thereof." As to the form of admission to the benefice, the Church courts are left at perfect liberty to exercise their own discretion. But it is clear they could not use, and never have used, the old ceremonial of induction.' 'It may be true,' the Lord President continued, ' that the old name of the ceremony of induction still lingers in the common speech of the country, and may be used popularly even in the proceedings of Church courts as an equivalent of "admission to a benefice." It is remarkable, however, that in the earlier authoritative or *quasi*-authoritative Church documents, as distinguished from Acts of Parliament, the term "induction" entirely disappeared. In the First and Second Books of Discipline, in Pardovan's *Collections*, in Principal Hill's *View of the Constitution of the Church of Scotland*, "admission of ministers" and not "induction" is the phrase used. But what is the act of admitting a minister to a benefice, and what is its effect? There is no *actus solemnis* apart from ordination. By the imposition of the hands of the Presbytery, the candidate is admitted and set apart to the office of the holy ministry. If he has been already ordained the fact is minuted. What follows is not a ceremony at all, but merely a recognition of the new minister as a member of Presbytery in his capacity of minister of the benefice to which he has been presented or elected.'[1]

[1] 'Institution was formerly given by the presiding Presbyter delivering to the newly ordained pastor the pulpit Bible, and by putting into his hands the key of the church and the bell-strings. This was done at the

His enjoyment of the benefices of both classes is in its nature absolute, qualified only by the condition of dutifully serving the cure to which the benefices are attached. Resignation, deposition, or transportation may terminate his tenure as well as death; he is not, then, strictly even a liferenter (but he may be enrolled on a valuation roll as such in respect of his manse and glebe).

It is the duty of the minister to preserve his benefices for his successors in the cure, but even his cession of any of his rights enjoyed as minister will not affect those who come after him. The minister of Falkland gave up, with concurrence of the Presbytery, his manse and glebe (in 1650) for an annual payment; but in 1793 the Court found one of the ministers of Falkland entitled to a manse and glebe (*Minister of Falkland* v. *Johnston*, 1793, M. 5155; see also *Panmure* v. *Presbytery of Brechin* (Brechin), Dec. 12, 1855, 18 D. 197).

To this rule there is one exception: where the minister has accepted £20 Scots in place of 'minister's grass,' the bargain cannot afterwards be recalled (*Minister of Dollar* v. *Duke of Argyll*, 1807, M., Glebe, App. 7).

No minister can hold a plurality of benefices (Act 1584, c. 132); a cure consisting of parishes united in one parish does not constitute plurality.

Thirteen years' uninterrupted peaceable possession by an incumbent of a subject as his benefice, or a part of it, supports a presumptive right in his favour to continuance of possession without a written title. This is the rule of *Decennalis et Triennalis Possessio*, as recognised by the law of Scotland.

close of the service, as appears, for example, from the following extract from the Records of the Presbytery of Perth in 1700: "The moderator having closed the action with prayer and praise, give the said Mr. C. institution by delivering him the kirk Bible, key of the kirk doors, and bellstrings; whereupon Mr. C. for his part, and J. B., elder, in name of the rest of the elders and parishioners, asked and took instruments in the clerk's hands."'—Sprott, *Worship and Offices of the Church of Scotland* (1882), p. 215.

Seven years' possession by a minister also enables him without a title to retain, *qua* ecclesiastic, possession of a subject. A judgment following on such possession is regarded as in nature and effect merely possessory, while in the case of thirteen years' possession the judgment amounts to a discerniture that the subject so possessed belongs to and forms part of the benefice, and to this effect operates as a written title of property in the subject.

Stipend is subject, by the Act 1669, *c.* 9, to a quinquennial prescription, unless proved by writ or oath. A right to stipend is acquired by uninterrupted payment for forty years to the occupant of a cure of stipend (*Boswell* v. *Town of Kirkcaldy*, 1668, M. 10,890; *Minister of Eyemouth* v. *Officers of State*, 1756, M. 15,677; *Baird* v. *Minister of Polmont*, July 3, 1832, 10 S. 752).

Before a second minister can obtain a modification or augmentation of stipend there must be either a special agreement on the part of the heritors that his stipend be payable out of the teinds, or his appointment *qua* parish minister must be one made by the Parliamentary Commissioners or the Teind Court (*Falkirk* case, Dec. 31, 1707, Connell, *Parishes*, p. 121; *Elgin*, 1714, *ibid.* 129; *Old Machar*, *ibid.* 131; *Culross*, *ibid.* 133; *Marshall* v. *Town of Kirkcaldy*, 1738, M. 14,795; *Fairnie* v. *Heritors of Dunfermline*, M. 14,796; *Inveraray* case, Connell, 146; *Buist* v. *Cheape* (St. Andrews), June 5, 1822, S.T., 23; *Magistrates of Haddington* v. *Kennedy*, Mar. 15, 1859, 21 D. 734).

A minister's stipend is attachable for debt. No portion of it is alimentary, but a minister will be allowed to keep enough to make an alimentary provision sufficient to enable him to discharge the duties of the cure, even against creditors (*Minister of Linton* v. *Creditors*, 136, cited in *Smith* v. *Earl of Moray* (Petty), Dec. 13, 1815, F.C.; *A. B.*, Petitioner, Nov. 26, 1823, 2 S. 526; *A. B.* v. *Sloan*, June 30, 1824, 3 S. 195; *Learmonth* v. *Paterson*, Jan. 21, 1858, 20 D. 418). A minister who was assistant and successor to a parish minister had emoluments of £106 a year, and debts amounting to £1100. He applied for *cessio*, and it was held by the First Division of the Court of Session that he was entitled to the benefit of *cessio* on his assigning £20 a year to his creditors. Lord Shand, however, observed that if the minister applied for his discharge, it might be fairly argued that, in view of his income being certainly increased in the event of his surviving the present parish minister, a larger sum on his death should be provided (*Simpson* v. *Jack*, Nov. 23, 1888, 16 R. 131).

Income-tax is payable upon all stipend, even if a portion of it is applied to the salary of an assistant, although the 52nd section of the Income-Tax Act of 1853 provides that, in assessing the tax on any minister, it shall be lawful to deduct from his profits any sums of money paid or expenses incurred by him 'necessarily in the performance of his duty.' It was held that this provision applied only to expenses incurred by a minister in the personal performance of his duty, and did not apply to a sum of money contributed by a minister, who from his age required the services of an assistant, to make up that assistant's salary to a certain fixed sum, the rest of which was raised by the congregation (*Lothian* v. *Macrae* (Hawick), Dec. 12, 1884, 12 R. 336).

A minister's right to stipend terminates with his death, deposition, resignation, or transportation to another charge. If the interest in the benefice ceases before 15th May (Whitsunday), he receives no part of the stipend of the year's crop; if between 15th May and 29th September (Michaelmas) he receives one-half; if after 29th September he receives the whole stipend (Stair, ii. 8, 33; Erskine, ii. 10, 54). While the right to stipend by ministers is regulated by these terms, as the stipend periodically accruing (except when modified in money) is derived from the year's crop when reaped, so the year's stipend does not become exigible. This is because theoretically the stipend has no existence until the arrival of the latter term.

In cases where an assistant and successor has been appointed to a parish minister, he succeeds, on the removal of the incumbent, to the enjoyment of the benefice without fresh induction. In the other cases above mentioned *vacant* stipend may be found due.

A proprietor who has a bare superiority over lands, or one who has a security right over lands, on which no possession has followed, and who has not intromitted with the fruits, is not liable for minister's stipend (*Jackson* v. *Cochrane* (Cupar-Fife), Feb. 27, 1873, 11 Mac. 475), for it is intromission with crop that renders a proprietor liable for stipend (see Lord Cowan in *University of Glasgow* v. *Pollok*, May 27, 1868, 6 Mac. 884).

A Presbytery may legally admit and ordain a minister of the Church of Scotland, and thereby entitle him to stipend, without his taking any oath of allegiance, abjuration, or making any declaration in lieu thereof, or subscribing 'the assurance' (*Bell* v. *Presbytery of Meigle* (Persie, *q.s.*), July 20, 1869, 7 Mac. 1083).

Minister's Ann or *Annat* is the half-year's stipend payable for the vacant half-year after the death of a minister, and to which his family or nearest of kin have right. This provision for ministers' relatives was of German origin. In Saxony, in the end of the sixteenth century, the custom was to allow the widow and children of a minister a grace of a half-year's salary; in other parts to allow a year's grace; and to secure this, the church, in many places, was kept vacant for the year, and the cure served by a neighbour. King James VI. is said to have made ann the subject of a letter to the General Assembly in 1595. The letter is lost. The Act passed by the Assembly on June 28, 1595, is as follows: 'Anent the Act made in favour of the Executors of ministers, the Assembly and brethren foresaid for cleiring thereof declares, if the minister die after Michaelmas, *quia fruges separatæ sunt a solo*, that his executors sall fall that yeir's rent and the half of the nixt.' It is pointed out by the Lord President (Inglis), in giving judgment in the case of *St. John's*, Edinburgh, that the Act in favour of the minister's executors referred to is the Act 1571, *c.* 41—an Act in favour of ecclesiastics who fall fighting against the king's enemies, giving them and their nearest of kin, not only the fruits on the ground, with the ann thereafter, but also the next presentation to the benefice. 'That Act is intended for a different Church and clergy,' said the Lord President, 'and for very different circumstances altogether, and there is not much light to be got from it. We find King James VI., however, taking the matter up again after the re-establishment of Episcopacy.' This appears from the *Peterhead* case of 1626. 'In a double poinding at the instance of the Earl Marischal, who was charged by the relict and bairns of the deceased minister of Peterhead, who was incumbent and served the cure, and who died before the feast of Michaelmas anno 1623, and who was on the other part charged by the new entrant minister for the stipend of the year 1624; to the which stipend for the whole year the said entrant minister craved the only right, and alleged that he ought to be answered thereof for both the terms of Whitsunday and Martinmas that year, in respect he served the cure that whole year; and the relict and bairns of the deceased minister claiming right to the half of that year's stipend, by reason of an Act and Statute of the Kirk, introduced in favour of the relicts and bairns of deceased prelates and ministers, which appoints the duties of the half of the profits of the prelacy and siclike of the stipend for the year subsequent next after the decease of the incumbent, to pertain to the relict and bairns of the said deceased incumbent, and the other half to pertain only to the entrant: The Lords having seen and considered an ordinance and Act made by the bishops which had relation to a letter of the deceased King James tending and written for that same effect, and which was engrossed in the said Act, and which Act was produced by the said entrant minister; by the which Act it was found that when the prelate dies before the Michaelmas, and after the Whitsunday, that his relict and heirs shall have that year's profits and rents of the benefice, both the Whitsunday and Martinmas terms thereof that year, and nothing of the year subsequent; and if the prelate die after the Michaelmas, that his relict and heirs shall have right to the half of the profits and rents of the subsequent year beside, and attain the whole rents of that year when he dies,' the Court gave effect to the Act (*The Earl Marischal v. The Relict and Bairns of the Minister of Peterhead*, July 19, 1626, 1 Br. Sup. 36). The case of *Fairley's Executors* (July 5, 1662), M. 472, is inconsistent with this, but the guiding statute is the Act 1672, c. 13. It provides, 'that in all cases hereafter the ann shall be an half-year's rent of the benefice or stipend over and above what is due to the defunct for his incumbency, which is now settled to be thus, viz. :—If the incumbent survive Whitsunday, there shall belong to them for their incumbency the half of that year's stipend or benefice, and for the ann the other half; and if the incumbent survive Michaelmas he shall have right to that whole year's rent for his incumbency, and for his ann shall have the half-year's rent of the following year; and that the executors shall have right thereto without necessity or expenses of a confirmation.' Payments of stipend and ann under the Act 1672 are not affected by the Apportionment Act, 1870, 33 and 34 Vict. c. 35 (*Latta (Fraser's Trustee)* v. *Edinburgh Ecclesiastical Commissioners* (St. John's, Edinburgh), Nov. 30, 1877, rev. judgment of Lord Ordinary (Curriehill), 5 R. 266). It was provided in an agreement between the parish minister of Penicuik and his assistant and successor that the former should 'surrender' to the latter £165 of the annual income derivable from the benefice of said parish, payable half-yearly at Martinmas and Whitsunday. The minister died on 29th April 1887, unmarried. The First Division of the Court of Session held that under the agreement the minister's executor was not bound to pay the assistant for his services between the previous Martinmas and that day, the stipend for that period being payable to the minister's next-of-kin, as annat, and there having been no personal obligation upon him and his representatives to make any payment (*Dow* v. *Imrie* (Penicuik), July 15, 1887, 14 R. 928).

By 50 Geo. III. *c.* 54, executors or personal representatives of ministers whose stipends are augmented to £150 under the Act are entitled, § 16, to one half-yearly moiety of the augmentation to be so granted in name of ann, over and above the stipend due to the deceased minister, in the same manner as in ordinary stipends : and the Barons of Exchequer are empowered to grant precepts for payment of this ann to those having right thereto, on their receipt, without confirmation or making up any other titles. The Act 5 Geo. IV. *c.* 90 (June 21, 1824), as to churches in the Highlands, provides, § 24, that the widow or nearest of kin of a minister of a church under the Act shall be entitled to the same payments as those of the parochial clergy.

When a minister leaves a widow and children, one-half of the ann is payable to the widow and one-half to the children, who share *per capita* (*Children of Macdermit*, 1747, M. 464); when there are no children, one-half falls to the widow and one-half to the minister's nearest of kin ; when there is no widow, but children, they take all. If there be neither widow nor children, the nearest of kin take the ann.

Ann is not included in the inventory of a deceased minister's estate for confirmation (Act 1672). Ann is given the minister 'on such conditions that it can never form part of his executry estate, for it is never *in bonis* of the defunct; but that only enhances the value of the gift, for his widow and children will always have a claim to it preferable to the claims of his creditors' (Lord President (Inglis), *Latta's* case, *supra*, 1272).

(2) A minister of a landward, or landward-burghal, parish enjoys, so long as he fills the cure, the liferent of a manse, the size and comforts of which are not readily determinable by any standard save that of Lord Kinloch (*Heritors of Insch* v. *Storie*, Dec. 18, 1869, 8 Mac. 369), that 'the manse of the minister should be the dwelling-house of a gentleman.' The manse should have a stance of an acre, stable, barn, byre, garden, etc. The up-keep and repair of the manse is a burden upon the heritors, unless the manse has been declared 'free.' The minister is entitled to have a garden wall. That a minister may *let* his manse for a short period was decided in the case of *Aberdour*, where the minister for several years had let his manse furnished for two months in summer while he took his family to another part of the country for change of air. The duties of the parish were discharged by a substitute who did not reside in the manse, and the minister came occasionally to preach on Sundays. The heritors having raised an action against the minister, concluding for declarator that he had no right to let the manse, and for interdict against his doing so, the Court held that, as the letting of the manse did not injure it, the heritors had no interest or title to interfere (*Heritors of Aberdour* v. *Roddick*, Dec. 14, 1871, 10 Mac. 221). The Lord Justice-Clerk (Moncreiff) observed: 'I do not think the heritors have any title to insist in this declarator, apart from their interest as liable to maintain the building. They are not proprietors of the manse. Neither are they, in any sense, the trustees of the property. In virtue of their resulting obligation they have a title to see that the property is duly administered with a view to its being kept in repair. But they have nothing more; they have no right beyond this to interfere in any way with the minister's possession or administration. Their right in the church and churchyard stands on an entirely different footing, for as regards them the minister has no patrimonial interest in either, and the heritors

have the property as administrators-in-trust. But a minister's right to his manse and glebe is entirely otherwise. He is more than occupant. He represents and administers for the series of incumbents who are collectively the proprietors. He cannot affect the interest of his successors ; but subject to this condition he has all the rights of a proprietor, at least so far as necessary for the complete enjoyment of the subject for the period of his incumbency. . . . His right is precisely of the same kind as his right to the glebe. I give no opinion as to how far the minister can virtually alienate the manse during his incumbency, or let it for a prolonged term to his own exclusion. I can conceive cases in which this might not be an unreasonable exercise of his power. I can also conceive cases in which it would be entirely inadmissible.'

(3) He is entitled to a glebe of at least four acres of arable ground, or sixteen soums of pasture land, and to minister's grass, *i.e.* land sufficient to provide grazing for two milk cows and a horse. He does not appear to be entitled to ask for a wall round the glebe from the heritors. He may lease his glebe under certain conditions, or feu it (29 and 30 Vict. *c.* 71).

(4) He is not liable in payment of poor-rates. See *Hogg* v. *Parochial Board of Auchtermuchty*, June 22, 1880, 7 R. 986.

(5) He receives from £8 to £20 annually for providing Communion elements. If the minister fails to administer the sacrament at least once annually, or does not expend the whole sum, the balance ought to be applied to pious purposes, *e.g.* the relief of the poor, and the heritors may compel the minister to apply it (*Heritors of Abdie* v. *Corsan*, 1713, M. 2490 ; *Heritors of Strathmiglo* v. *Gillespie*, 1742, M. 2491). When there are no surplus teinds the Court will not award a sum against the heritors. If a party voluntarily undertakes to supply Communion elements, his liability is only for so much as may be required, although by a custom for a term of years a greater quantity may have been provided (*Buchanan* v. *Magistrates of Dunbar* (Dunbar), Feb. 26, 1869, 6 S.L.R. 381).

The heritors provide the Communion vessels, etc. By the Act 1617, *c.* 6, it was provided that all parish churches should be provided (1) with basins and lavoirs for the administration of the sacrament of Baptism, and (2) cups, tables, and table-cloths for Communion. These were to be provided between June 1617 and February 1618 by the parishioners, usually understood here to mean heritors. The vessels, etc., were committed to the charge of the parish minister; he, his heirs and executors, are answerable for their loss or profanation (*Hamilton* v. *Minister of Cambuslang,* 1752, M. 10,570).

(6) A clergyman who is also a Dean of the Chapel-Royal receives a share of the teinds of the Chapel-Royal of Stirling.

While from time to time reference has been made to vicarage or lesser tithes, the reader's attention in the preceding pages has been chiefly directed to rectorial or greater tithes. Vicarage tithes, indeed, continued to be paid after the Reformation, and are still calculable when they are traced; but the right to them is lost by disuse for forty years, while the right to parsonage or rectorial teinds is not lost by desuetude. Whales were teinded among vicarage tithes, and certain salmon-fishings have been held to be subject to valuation.[1]

Berwickshire fish teinds were commuted by the Act 27 and 28 Vict. *c.* 23, and a similar claim as regards Leith by 55 and 56 Vict. *c.* 177. Vicarage teinds seem to have been generally, if not always, local; so that the canon rule *decimæ debentur parocho* applied more really than in the case of the parsonage teinds. While teinds were defined by the canonists to be of three classes—*personal*, as of profits of personal industry; *prædial*, as of the natural fruits of the ground or water; and *mixed*, the industrial fruits of the ground only—we have noted *supra* (p. 34) that personal teinds are very rarely mentioned

---

[1] Elliot, *Teind Court Procedure,* p. 76.

in Scottish records. Stair says: 'Our custom alloweth of no personal teinds' (*Institutions*, bk. ii. tit. viii. 6).

In concluding this account of teinds, it will be noticed that had the valuations introduced by Charles I. been carried out all over the kingdom, the position of parties would have been very different from what it now is. At the present day there may be in one parish: (1) lands not liable in payment of teinds, as held under titles *cum decimis inclusis*; (2) lands of which the teinds were valued in the reign of Charles I., and then purchased, and lands of which the teinds were valued at any time from 1627, but have not been purchased; (3) lands of which the teinds were, say, last year valued and purchased on calculations based on a very different rental; (4) lands of which the teinds have never been valued. It is highly desirable that the valuation of all teinds should be completed as speedily as possible, whether they are purchased or not. Until such a valuation is made, it is quite impossible to say what the value of the teinds of Scotland is. It is, perhaps, little surprising that there should be much popular misconception as to when tithes are payable. They are not universal over Scotland in the sense that all lands are in the same position as regards tithe-paying. They are not of fixed or equal proportions relatively to the rental of lands or their productiveness. In some parishes the teinds are exhausted, in others they are not. There is, in short, no possibility of laying down any general proposition relative to teinds which will be at once adequate and easily intelligible. When we look at the payment of tithes as conceived by the Early Christian Church, on the one hand, and on the other the complicated machinery which in Scotland to-day is supposed to work out results similar, as regards the maintenance of clergy, to those sought to be obtained by that primitive Church, something little short of despair seizes the mind of any one who attempts to explain the historical relationship of the one to the other. Without historical inquiry the modern law of teinds is incomprehensible, and even with the aid of history it requires patience and some study to arrive at an explanation of the curious anomalies with which that law presents us. If the writer has succeeded in at least providing the students of ecclesiastical history and of historical law with a lantern along a very obscure and dusky passage, his object will have been achieved, although he may warn them that no lantern will render personal investigation, and much careful picking of footsteps, unnecessary.[1]

---

[1] The following books will be found useful by those who desire to pursue the study of teinds further. The editions named are those which have been used by the author :—

Bellesheim, Alphonse, *History of the Catholic Church in Scotland*, ii. 1887, iii. 1889.
Buchanan, Wm., *Treatise on the Law of Scotland on the subject of Teinds or Tithes*, 1863.
Bryce, Jas., *The Holy Roman Empire* (7th ed.), 1880.
Connell, Sir John, *A Treatise on the Law of Scotland respecting Tithes*, 1815.
Elliot, Nenion: (1) *Teinds or Tithes and Procedure in the Court of Teinds in Scotland*, 1893 ; (2) *Teind Papers*, 1874.
Freeman, Edw. A., *History of the Norman Conquest in England* (2nd ed.), 1870, vol. i.
Froude, J. A., 'Annals of an English Abbey,' in *Short Studies on Great Subjects*, vol. iii., 1888.
Innes, Cosmo, *Origines Parochiales Scotiae*, 1851-55.
  ,, ,, *Lectures on Scotch Legal Antiquities*, 1872.
  ,, ,, *Sketches of Early Scotch History*, 1861.
Kirkwood, Anderson, 'On the Law of Teinds in Scotland,' Art. in *Journal of Jurisprudence*, vol. xvi., 1872.
Milton, John, *Considerations touching the likeliest means to remove Hirelings out of the Church, wherein is also Discourse of Tithes*, etc.
Robertson, E. William, *Scotland under her Early Kings*, 2 vols., 1862.
  ,, ,, *Historical Essays in connection with the Land, the Church*, etc., 1877.
Robertson, Jos., 'Scottish Abbeys and Cathedrals,' Art. in *Quarterly Review*, lxxxv., 1849.

Selborne, Earl of, *Ancient Facts and Fictions concerning Churches and Tithes*, 1888.
Selden, John, *The Historie of Tithes*, 1618.
Skene, W. F., *Celtic Scotland*, vol. ii. 'Church and Culture,' 1877.
Stair, Lord, *Institutions of the Law of Scotland*, ed. by J. S. More, 1832.
Story, Rev. R. H., D.D., *The Church of Scotland Past and Present*, N.D.
Spotswood, J., *History of the Church and State in Scotland* (4th ed.), 1677.
Stubbs, Bishop, *Constitutional History of England*, 3 vols., 1880.
Thorpe, B., *Ancient Laws and Institutes of England*, vol. i., 1840.

CHAPTER VI

THE SURVIVAL OF THE OLD CHURCH

The differing characteristics of the three kingdoms are curiously illustrated by the effect of the Reformation in each. In England, the form taken by the Reformed Church is frequently called Episcopalian—not in itself a good term, for the Church of Rome was Episcopalian too, but significant of the fact that of two forms of Church government denying the supremacy of the Roman pontiff the English nation preferred that which provided for diocesan superintendence by bishops. In Scotland the national preference for the Presbyterian form was as markedly shown, for the occasional intervals of Episcopal government in Scotland were as meaningless as was the interval of Presbyterianism in England. The non-Episcopacy of the Protectorate days serves as a convenient contrast to the Episcopacy which with that exception is uninterrupted from the reign of Elizabeth to that of Victoria. The non-Presbyterianism of James VI. and Charles I. in like manner, but the clearer marks out the Presbyterianism of Scotland from Mary's reign till now. In Ireland the Church of Rome sat firm, but was Reformed within herself, and the Episcopal Church, which the Government long recognised, was as little the Church of the people as a whole as was the vigorous Presbyterian Church of Antrim and the north.

Now that Ireland, like the United States, has no Established Church, she completes the circle of contrasts. In England, the Presbyterians and Roman Catholics are dissenters; in Scotland, the Roman Catholics and Episcopalians are dissenters; in Ireland, Presbyterians, Episcopalians, and Roman Catholics are all on the same level, but, practically, Presbyterians and Episcopalians are, as regards the bulk of the population, dissenters there. Thus the effect of the Reformation in the three countries is seen in each in a different way. As the peoples of the three kingdoms are different, so are the forms of their religion.

In large measure the ultimate adoption of one mode of Church government over another was political. To the Englishman the Church of Henry VIII., of Edward VI., of Elizabeth, was a symbol of political protest against the notion that any but Englishmen should bear rule in England; in Scotland Presbyterianism meant as clearly that no English custom favoured by the later Stuarts should overcome the Scottish preference for the early Church of the Reformers; and in Ireland, during centuries, the Church of Rome, recruited from the ranks of the Irish peasantry, stood out to Ireland's wandering sons as the only truly national thing left to Erin. Thus, looked at from the lowest point of view, the Church of each country was its political symbol. It is still so in Ireland; Presbyterianism is still so in Scotland; and if it is not so in England, it is because England, the largest and richest partner of the concern, has grown so contented, or so forgetful, as to fail to recall how in the old days the history of the Protestant Church and her own were identical.

Reflections such as these are suggested by the perusal of the *History of the Catholic Church in Scotland*, by Dr. Bellesheim, Canon of Aix-la-Chapelle, which has been translated into English by Father Oswald Hunter-Blair, and to which frequent reference has been made in the preceding chapters.

It is of great service to have the facts relative to the old Scottish Church clearly and succinctly stated from the Catholic point of view, especially by one who is so far removed from Scottish environment as to be able to view Scottish politics and Scottish sects from a point which is comparatively neutral. Canon Bellesheim's *History* may with profit be read in company with Principal Lee's *Lectures on the History of the Church of Scotland*, from the period of Queen Mary's arrival in Scotland till her abdication. To read the Canon's work, one would scarcely suppose that a vigorous established Presbyterian Church was in existence from 1560, although in that year the Articles of the Confession were ratified by the three Estates; while the reader will seek in vain in the pages of many Presbyterian writers for any hint that during Mary's brief tenure of actual power the Pope was so little conscious of there having been a religious revolution in Scotland, that in 1562 he urged Mary to send bishops and an ambassador from Scotland to join in the deliberation of the Council of Trent.[1] This does not indicate that the historians of either party are wilfully partial to their own Church, or unfair to the other, but that Presbyterian and Catholic alike stick each to his appointed task, and consequently that in the work of the former the rapid rise of the Reformed Church stands out as the salient feature of the age, while in that of the latter it is the tenacity of the hold of the Catholic Church in Scotland which rivets the attention. One must welcome all the light possible about this puzzling chapter of Scottish religious history. *Which* was the Church of Scotland in King James's childhood depended entirely upon the mental standpoint of the Scotsmen of the day. Undoubtedly the Articles were ratified in 1560, but they were not recorded among the Acts of Parliament for some years afterwards. Again, among the members of Parliament who attended, and did not oppose the adoption of the

[1] The Pope had in the previous year sent Mary the Golden Rose, with a letter in which the Holy Father speaks of the Queen as of one 'who, like a most fair rose among thorns, diffuses far and wide the sweet odour of her faith and good works.'

Protestant confession, were very many of the leading Roman Catholic ecclesiastics of high rank. Their action is truly inexplicable, except upon the somewhat risky grounds suggested by Bellesheim, that they did not regard the Parliament as a legal one, the Estates having met without the Queen's writ. In that case they might surely have stayed away, or (like four of their number) they might as a precautionary measure have voted against the adoption of the new Articles. 'Considering that the manifesto of the Reformers was laid before the Parliament on August 5th,' says Bellesheim, 'and that the debate was not opened until the 17th, there would seem to have been amply sufficient time, not only to have studied this document, but to have prepared an effectual rejoinder to it.' The clergy apparently did not believe that the crisis was serious, or else they were so thoroughly satisfied with the prospect of retaining their livings for their lifetime without the necessity of undertaking any clerical labour, as to lean, politically, rather to the side of the Reformers, which afforded them the greatest chance of enjoying ease without work. This seems borne out by the answer of Mary herself to Nicholas Goudanus, the Papal Nuncio, who visited Scotland in 1562, when he spoke of the Papal letters he was instructed to deliver to the Scottish bishops,—that the Nuncio could only deliver them safely to the Bishop of Ross, who was President of the Court of Session. Ultimately, all the letters were handed to the Queen's private secretary. The Nuncio, under such circumstances, was scarcely likely to be favourably impressed by the clergy; and in his narrative he mentions how 'one day, close to the place where I lodged, three priests publicly abjured the Catholic faith; and another time, while I was there, one of the principal superintendents, a doctor of theology and a monk, then about seventy years of age, was openly married.'

In 1564 the Pope, still loftily ignoring that anything had happened to make his advice absurd, urged the Queen to dismiss all heretics from high offices of State, and desired the two metropolitans of Scotland to see that the Tridentine decrees were duly enforced, which it was manifestly impossible they could be, for the Archbishop of St. Andrews was in prison and he of Glasgow in exile. Yet Mary's marriage with Darnley was celebrated according to the ritual of the Roman Church; James VI. was baptized at Stirling according to the same ritual. Indeed, James himself, while he was King of Scots, was believed not to be wholly without leaning to the Church of Rome; but two excellent reasons told strongly against any open encouragment of that Church, the first being his desire to remain on the most friendly terms with Queen Elizabeth, and the other (as appears from a contemporary estimate of his character which Father Hunter-Blair translates in the appendix to vol. III. of Bellesheim's *History*) that he feared his title to the throne, and the prolongation of his reign, 'would be in the greatest jeopardy were the Supreme Pontiff to be restored to his former rights over the Church, and, as it were, to a share in the government of the realm, the King being deprived of his ecclesiastical jurisdiction, that is of half the powers he now enjoys; and this, he believes, would certainly follow, if he suffers the Catholics to grow and increase in numbers.' It does not appear nowadays that it would have made much difference had King James declared himself a Catholic. The Reformation had been too sweeping in its character to admit of being stopped by King James's displeasure. When it is considered how little effect the prelatic preferences of that King in his English days or of King Charles had upon the Scottish Church, it may safely be averred that the Roman Catholic form of religion, even if supported by the king, had little chance of being established again. No doubt there were very many in Scotland who were sincere Catholics long after the days of Knox. The religion of a nation is not changed in a day. The men of the Reformation had all been educated under the Catholic Church, and their orders were those of that Church. The Reformation in its inception, further, may be said, like most popular movements, to have come forth from the lower middle classes, or, more correctly, the upper lower classes. They were the class who contributed to the ordinary priesthood. The Church itself had long been conscious of the abuses in her midst, and so far as good resolutions went the leaders of the Church were determined on reform. Practical reform was, however, hopeless, because the nominal holders of so many Church offices were, as we have seen, laymen, bastards, or favourites of kings, men who monopolised the richest revenues and left the inferior offices badly paid or neglected. This was all very clear to the men who entered the priesthood. At that time, and for six hundred years previously, the only entrance to political life for a man who was not a noble was through the Church. It was almost the only liberal profession, and it monopolised the intellect of the age. By this monopoly the clergy controlled the politics of the kingdom. The nobles avenged themselves by taking clerical offices in many cases, so as the better to qualify for political influences, or to command the revenues which would further political ends; and as for the hungry sheep—they looked up and were not fed. The rotten state of the Church was very visible to two out of three social classes. The nobles saw in the Church an institution monopolising political power and with great revenues. The middle class, particularly those of it who entered the Church, saw that the intrusion of the nobility and the conversion of a sacred into a secular organisation made all true development of religious zeal or any adequate reforms of the Church impossible. The Reformation was therefore joyfully hailed by the two classes for very different reasons. The nobles saw politics emancipated from the skirts of the monk, and saw too the possibility of sharing in the division of the Church's patrimony which was almost inevitable; the loyal clergy, on the other hand, the men who groaned under the miserable mismanagement and apathy which characterised the Church during the long minorities of the Scottish kings and the disorders of their brief majorities, with gladness welcomed the light from over the sea which made religion once more a living thing in the land. No doubt both classes were deceived in each other. The politician did not look for the pious zeal for religion and education which distinguished Knox and his followers; nor, on the other hand, did the clergy expect that the nobles who had expressed solicitude for reformation were to appropriate the Church's revenues. Still, both classes knew what the Reformation was, or what each meant it to be, and had each too strong an interest in furthering its triumph to permit of allowing its enemies to reassert themselves. The politicians bore as well as they could the scoldings of the clergy—'old priest writ large,' indeed—comforted by their political emancipation, and the clergy, poverty-stricken and robbed though they knew the Church to be, counted that as little compared with the purity of administration and simplicity of worship which were the certain inheritance of God's people in Scotland. But there was a third great class, the men and women who lived in quiet villages in distant counties, to whom politics had no meaning, to whom the Church was all the intellectual life they knew, who had been baptized by priests and married by priests, and hoped to receive the last communion from priestly hands. News travelled slowly in those days, and that there should be confusion of tongues in Edinburgh, or a battle lost near Glasgow, was no reason why, in the islands of Argyll or the hills of Aberdeenshire, the priest should be sent packing. The Reformation in Scotland, no doubt, was nominally accomplished with some rapidity, so far as the State *qua* State was concerned; but it took a long time before the Presbyterian form of worship actually replaced the Roman Catholic form in the country places. A change of Church government so vital did not come into operation with the swiftness of a modern Act of Parliament creating a school board in each parish or a council in each county. Not, indeed, that even those are fair subjects for comparison; for after all they are purely civil changes, whereas the change wrought by the Reformation, so far as country folks went, was mainly that of doctrine and ritual, and in many places the people were content enough with the old ways.

We may pass by the record of the Church of Rome in Scotland, from James's succession to the English throne to the time of Queen Anne, without remark. No period of Scotland's religious history is so well known. The persecutions of Covenanters, the rabbling of curates, the see-saw of Presbyterianism and Episcopacy bear the most momentous evidence to the fact that Scotland had at least turned her back upon Rome. There were still many noble families who remained Catholic—still more who were but Protestants in name; but the country was undoubtedly lost to the Pope. The hierarchy ceased to be; Propaganda did not intermit interest in Scottish affairs, but it was the interest taken in a heathen land. Emissaries were from time to time despatched from Italy to report upon the state of things political and religious in Scotland; and with no little danger to themselves—for each priest's head meant a high reward—they gave in their perfectly frank and thoroughly honest reports on the desperate state of the realm of the Stuarts; Rome has ever been well informed.

In the first years of the eighteenth century the Roman Catholic form of religion was almost extinct in Scotland. Masters were forbidden to employ Catholics even in domestic service, and the hunt for priests was vigilant and unceasing, five hundred marks being offered by the Privy Council to any one apprehending a priest. A return of 'Popish parents and their children in various districts of Scotland, as given in to the Lords of the Privy Council and to the Commission of the General Assembly, 1701 to 1705' (Maitland Club publications) assigns 160 Catholics to

Edinburgh, five to Leith, twelve to Glasgow, and twenty to Perth. In the Highlands and Islands, however, things were different. South Uist and Barra, Canna, Rum, and Muck were entirely Popish. In Knoydart and Moray there were only four Protestants, in Arisaig, Moydart, and Glengarry but one. In all there were about 4500 Catholics, with six priests, while there were only five Protestant ministers, in the whole bounds of Skye Presbytery. The Jacobite rising of 1715 caused the few Catholics of the North to be subjected to fresh sufferings; but Bishop Nicholson, who, dressed as a layman, discharged with great difficulty and danger the duties of Scottish vicar-apostolic, was able to found the little seminary of Scalan, on the Braes of Glenlivat, a secluded spot, only accessible by a bridle-path. In 1730, while the report to Propaganda was that the increase in the number of Catholics was considerable, it is mentioned with grief that persecution is so rife that the people are often by force and blows compelled to enter the Protestant churches. Bishop Macdonald in 1745 knew the state of the Highlands very much better than the Continental advisers of Prince Charles, and when the prince landed, he urged him to return at once to France. The Prince refused to desert the followers who gathered to greet him, and the disapproving prelate was carried to Glenfinnan to bless the royal standard. Of course, the defeat of Culloden was signal for a fresh persecution of the Catholics. The bishop fled to France, but returned four years later under the pseudonym of 'Mr. Brown' to continue his ministrations as best he could. The vineyard had indeed been well-nigh destroyed. Besides the Highlanders who fell in battle, a thousand had been transported to America, the Catholic chapels were destroyed, the little seminary at Scalan plundered, and the missals and vestments publicly burned. Nor did the fever soon cease. In 1755 'Mr. Brown' was arrested, and on 1st March 1756 the High Court of Justiciary at Edinburgh, in punishment for his refusal to 'purge himself of Popery,' sentenced him to banishment for life under pain of death if he returned to Scotland. This seems to have been the end of the matter; he was never again out of Scotland, he was not kept in prison, but quietly discharged his episcopal functions in the Highlands until his death seventeen years afterwards.[1] In 1770 the Catholics of South Uist were subjected to such active interference, however, that Bishop Hay raised subscriptions to defray the cost of transporting the entire people to America; and in 1802 the same prelate thought the best thing to do with the Catholics who had formed the 'Glengarry Fencibles,' on their being disbanded, was to procure their settlement in Canada. In 1800 the number of Catholic churches in Scotland was twelve, with three bishops and forty priests. During the first quarter of this century an enormous increase in the number of adherents took place. The 1000 Catholics of Edinburgh and Leith of 1800 had become 14,000 in 1829, and similar increases had taken place all over the country. The great modern development of the Roman Church did not, however, begin until the Catholic Emancipation Act was passed in 1829. It cannot be said it was the wish of Scotland that the Act should pass, when we read that 18,000 persons in Edinburgh and 37,000 in Glasgow petitioned against it; but Sir Walter Scott, Dr. Chalmers, Lords Jeffrey and Cockburn were on the side of religious freedom and tolerance. With one bound the Church sprang forward, although its great increase of members is due principally to the huge influx of Irishmen to Glasgow and the towns of the West of Scotland.

[1] Glengarry and Barra figure in Dr. Bellesheim's pages in strange disproportion to their modern importance. There was, however, even in the bitter times of 1675, a Catholic school in each place—the only Catholic schools in the Highlands. It is grimly suggestive of the Pope's real knowledge of Scotland to read that 'Propaganda would appear to have been disposed at first to insist on Catholic children being sent to those schools *from all parts of Scotland*'! Minster, the prefect of the then Catholic Mission, however, assured the Cardinals that Catholic parents would as soon send their children to Jamaica as to the island of Barra. Perhaps then the maps were searched for that lonely place.

With the restoration of the hierarchy in 1878 the present history of the Church ends. The restoration seems to have been due in great measure to the attitude of the Episcopal Church in Scotland, regarding which Dr. Bellesheim is remarkably frank :—

'It was on the members of this body that the erection of a true ecclesiastical hierarchy might be expected to make the most forcible impression. Their numbers amounted to some 55,000, nearly all belonging to the better classes, and in consequence possessed of considerable influence. A section of the body was known to approximate both in doctrine and in ritual observance to the forms of the Catholic Church; and it seemed as though before long there would be but one point of difference between Catholics and themselves—namely, the obedience which the former rendered and the latter refused to the Holy See. Under these circumstances the revival of a national hierarchy was greatly to be desired; and indeed, if they retained any longer than was absolutely necessary ecclesiastical designations borrowed from heathen countries,[1] the effect, especially on recent converts, could not be but highly detrimental, and might lead to consequences whose extent it was impossible to foresee' (vol. iv. pp. 301, 302).

We have now rapidly surveyed the history of the Roman Catholic Church in Scotland since it ceased to be the Church of the people. It is interesting, however, to inquire what remained of its ecclesiastical order in the parishes of Scotland. What did the Reformed Church keep of the elaborate parochial system which had been developed by the most diplomatic and far-sighted Church the world has ever known? The Reformers did not raze the tablets. Sometimes people speak as if they

---

[1] The titles of the bishops *in partibus infidelium* were strange. Bishop Chisholm was Bishop of Diocæsarea; Bishop Macdonald was Bishop of Acryndela; Bishop Gray was Bishop of Hypsopolis, and Bishop Lynch of Arcadiopolis. Eretria, Castabala, Parium, Anazarba, and Diana are amongst the simplest titles.

did. They did not map out fresh parishes, or destroy the parochial institutions; on the contrary, they took the Church as it was, and endeavoured with as little change as possible to modify the parochial system as it was in the pre-Reformation days into the system now familiar to us. A Presbytery replaced a bishop, a Synod an archbishop, and government by individuals gave place to government by committees. It is, however, when we wander into the domain of parochial ecclesiastical law that we find how few and slight, comparatively, were the changes made on that law by the Reformation—a subject, however, so large that we can only lightly touch upon it here.

The Reformation, with all its noise, made, as we have seen, little difference in the quiet country places; it made scarcely any upon the parochial law of the Church, even though the Church lost more than two-thirds of her endowments, and for years was crippled by her great needs. The law, so far as regarded the maintenance of the church and manse, knew little change. What change there was was due to the Church's poverty, which could not well contest the claims of the heritors or landowners to ownership of the Church lands, since those landowners were required to provide the money for its buildings and their repair. The old days when the minister was solemnly 'inducted' into his church, and received the Bible and the church keys as signs of his authority, passed away; the kirk-session took charge of the order of divine service, and the grumbling landowners kept the keys; the minister became (what he is now) merely a ministrant in an edifice over which he has no shadow of control.

Wretched churches, many of them, must have been those in which the preachers of the Reformation and of the century following met their flocks. They were small, often thatched, but seldom water-tight, with earthen floors, and windows which as a rule were not glazed and had to be closed in case of stormy weather. The men of the congregation stood about as they best might, the women brought their 'creepies' with them, or squatted on the floor with their plaids over their heads. The children played and ran about the church when they escaped their elders' eye, for more often than not the building was their week-day school-room, with which they were but too familiar. There were few pews in Scottish Churches until the middle of the seventeenth century, for up to the time of frequent and long sermons no seats were needed. When the Holy Communion was partaken of, forms were placed in the church; or if the space was insufficient, the sacrament was celebrated in the graveyard. Two of the most significant changes in the ritual after the Reformation were of course the tendering of the wine, as well as of the bread, to the people, and that all partook sitting reverently together; those were matters of ceremonial not without their influence on the economy of the Church, but outside the Church the old laws of the parish still guided the people. Generation has passed after generation into forgetfulness, but those laws—some of them little fitted for modern days—still regulate parish affairs. The Legislature has now and again stepped in to alter this or that ancient custom, to reduce the law as to the repair of churches and manses to something like order, as by the Ecclesiastical Buildings Act of 1868—a task but partially successful—or to place the control of the parish school in new hands, as by the Education Act of 1871; but as a rule the parochial ecclesiastical law of Scotland still rests on the law of the pre-Reformation Church of Scotland, and it is not surprising that some of it should seem out of date. The Church government by Kirk-sessions, Presbyteries, Synods, and Assembly is simple, and not liable to much misunderstanding. But when we turn to the position of the Church and the minister in their relation to the parishioners, the matter is not so clear.

In every parish we find a church. Who pays for the maintenance of that church? The answer would usually be the heritors, *i.e.* the proprietors of land in the parish. But this would depend, to begin with, on what kind of parish the church is situated in. In a parish *quoad sacra* (that is, a parish which has parochial boundaries only for ecclesiastical purposes, and not for civil purposes, such as education, relief of the poor, etc.) there is no burden on the heritor to maintain the church. That must be done by the congregation. But every *quoad sacra* parish is part of a larger and older parish, *quoad omnia*, and for the maintenance of its church every heritor is liable.

But how and to what extent is the heritor liable? He pays assessments, it will be answered, on the valuation of his lands within the parish. True, but there may be two ways of assessing heritors; they may be assessed on the 'valued rent,' a computation of values in Scots money which originated during the Protectorate, or they may be assessed on the 'real rent,' *i.e.* the rent as appearing from the valuation roll of the year of assessment. The amounts are, of course, ridiculously different, but the sum actually obtained is not in any way affected by the methods of computation. When an assessment is imposed on the 'valued rent,' it is imposed at the rate of so many shillings sterling per pounds Scots; when it is imposed on the real rent, it is imposed at the rate of so many pence per pound sterling. When an assessment *may* and when an assessment *must* be imposed on either the one scale or the other, are matters depending purely on circumstances—such as whether the church was built and the seats therein allocated among valued rent heritors prior to 1868. The law of the subject must be extricated from dozens of contradictory cases.

When we have arrived at this, that the Church must be maintained (in a rural district at least) by the heritors on the real or the valued rent-roll, we may safely affirm that the *Church* is the *property* of the heritors. This is established law. But what of the churchyard? Of course it is also under the heritors' control? Before that question can be answered, we must know whether the churchyard was in use before the year 1560 or not. If it was, then the heritors are absolute proprietors of the churchyard in a fiduciary character for the parish. If it is a churchyard of later date, then there is also a *quasi*-ownership in the families for whose burial-places certain lots have been apportioned; and it is not clear that the kirk-session have not also a voice in the matter, while in the case of a churchyard attached to a landward burghal parish the burgh magistrates also are not without jurisdiction.

From the church and the graveyard we pass on to the manse. Every parish has not a manse. A minister of a burghal parish is not entitled to one, neither is the minister of a parish *quoad sacra*. A minister of a country or landward parish is undoubtedly entitled to a manse; and by reading one Act of Parliament into another, and by a long series of decisions, the minister of a burghal landward parish has also secured his right to a manse.

We shall assume we are dealing with a country manse. Are the heritors liable for its upkeep? If they are liable for the church, they must be liable for the manse, it might be answered, for the manse is a pertinent of the church; there may be a church without a manse, but there can scarcely be a manse without a church. But the law has something to say about the manse as distinguished from the church. It may be a 'free manse.' If the heritors put the manse in a perfect state of repair, they are entitled to call upon the Presbytery to inspect the manse; and if the Presbytery is satisfied with the thoroughness of the work, the heritors are declared to be free from liability for the upkeep of the manse during their minister's incumbency. This is a delicate matter, for ministers are, as a rule, not very desirous of having a 'free manse,' when otherwise all the repairs would require to be paid for by the heritors. On the other hand, if the manse becomes 'free,' the heritors have an uncomfortable feeling that were the cure to become vacant by the 'call' of their minister to another parish, or by his death, the whole work of repair might require to be done over again, with the risk added that, the occupant of the 'free' manse having spent as little of his own money as he could, the probable state of the building would cause serious outlay to be incurred.

The imposition of heritors' assessments for the upkeep of church and manse is not at present entirely satisfactory. The system is full of anomalies, and is not devoid of abuses. The church is open to all the parish, for there are no seat rents (except in *quoad sacra* churches); the liability of the heritors for ecclesiastical assessments is independent of whether they go to the parish church or not. From time to time unpleasant scenes occur when dissenters refuse to pay those rates; and nothing is gained to the dignity of the National Church by petty squabbles about a few shillings—for the amount of the assessment is seldom a matter of much moment. Ecclesiastical assessments are irregular. They are not imposed annually, but only when the heritors (who themselves impose the assessment) are satisfied that money must be raised. The amount is generally inconsiderable if one regards the value of the heritor's property; and we never heard of a case where liability for such occasional assessments in the least affected the selling value of a property, or a purchaser's intention to buy. The desirableness of amending the incidence of ecclesiastical assessments is, however, scarcely questionable.

We have said above that no seat rents are chargeable except in *quoad sacra* parishes. This is perhaps sometimes forgotten, and parishioners are charged for their sittings. This is entirely against the law. There were no pews prior to the Reformation. The area of the church was free to the parishioners. By-and-bye permission was given to heritors to put up fixed seats or galleries or lofts in the church, so that particular persons or corporations should have comfortable accommodation. It is clear the kirk-session had nothing to do with the matter by law, for only the heritors can authorise or forbid alterations in the sacred edifice; but as a matter of convenience the kirk-session sometimes represented the heritors and gave the required leave. The appearance of a church with odd boards or pews here and there must have been very unseemly, and the next step was for the heritors to seat the entire church. Then the sittings thus provided were allocated amongst the heritors of the parish, so that each had seats for himself, his family, his tenants, and his servants Thus every class of person in a rural parish was provided for. The heritors' right to this accommodation is a matter of fixed law. How seat rents crept in, it is, however, not difficult to see. When the area of a church was once allocated, no reallocation was possible (this is still the law) until a new church was erected; but heritors died, lands changed hands, one man had no room for his tenants, another had too much, and the space of A. was taken by B. for hire. Corporations had far more sittings than they used, and even within recent times the occupiers have been charged with seat rents. Again, here and there a hamlet swelled into a large village, and artisans who were not heritors, nor servants, nor tenants, properly speaking, of heritors, required seats. Dissent was always causing little breaks in a congregation; the seats of the Auld Lichts were vacant in the parish church: what was to prevent the kirk-session turning an honest penny by letting those vacant seats to the artisans who (it was assumed) had no vested right to free seats? All this was totally wrong. Seat rents in parish churches are not legally chargeable, and never have been. Nor is the right of a heritor to his seat a right of exclusive occupancy, like his right to interment in the family burial-place in the graveyard. He has a right to accommodation only; if he does not use all the sittings allocated to him, they are free to any other parishioner. No heritor is entitled to let his seat for his own benefit; no kirk-session is entitled to let sittings; no heritor or kirk-session can sell sittings; and yet all those things have been done. One corporation till a few years ago used to spend the money it received as seat rent on an annual jovial supper! But magistrates in burghal parishes may legally let their allocated sittings if they apply the money to defraying the cost of church repairs; and heritors may sometimes even let their seats elsewhere if the rent is applied to the support of the poor, or to some other appropriate pious use within the parish. Such are the whims of the law; but we see that except in *quoad sacra* parishes, where pew rents are, by statute, leviable, the law is as it was before the Reformation, *i.e.* the area is free to all the parish for religious purposes, pews or no pews, whatever local custom may say to the contrary. The minister is paid by the stipend localled or charged upon the parish teinds, the church is maintained by the heritors, the relief of the poor is provided for by statute or by church-door collections; the church is for the people to worship in, free to all who can find room in it.

The above observations refer to landward or rural parishes only. In cities the difficulties attending the survival of the old parochial system are quite different. It is an essential of proper parochial government that the church and manse of a parish should be within that parish. The Roman Catholic Church in its 'missionary districts' (so it terms its parishes in Scotland), whenever it erects a church, builds adjoining it a house for clergy; and the priest lives there because he may be sent for at any moment. This is the true ideal of parochial government, for the people of a city have as much right to the comforting words of their minister as have rural parishioners. The custom of the Presbyterian city minister makes this too often impossible. He has no manse, and therefore has to provide himself with a house, and unfortunately he too often finds it outside the boundaries of his parish. The parishioners may or may not have a missionary in their midst. It is not too much to say that when clergymen undertake to serve the cure of a city parish they should live amongst its people; if a clergyman cannot fulfil his duties, he should not accept the charge of a parish. What the clergy of the Roman Catholic Church can do, the clergy of the Protestant Church of Scotland should be able to do. The law of the Church prior to the Reformation as to parochial residence was sometimes transgressed owing to the attractions of neighbouring religious houses and their cultivated society; but it was over and over again repeated by diocesan synod and by bishop that *a priest must reside in his parish.* This is still the law of Scotland. There is little wonder that the Roman Catholic Church, with its ministering servants resident among the people, ever ready to afford them the consolations of religion, is making strides in our great cities.[1]

The task of recapitulating the numerous instances in which pre-Reformation law or custom still regulate the parochial ecclesiastical law of Scotland is one which cannot be accomplished in a chapter. The Church in Scotland and the law relative to it have made several easily marked and easily known changes since allegiance to Rome was thrown off; but the broad rules which the Roman Church prescribed for the maintenance of the clergy by tithes and the ecclesiastical administration of the parish have proved as permanent as that Church herself, despite all the vicissitudes through which they have passed since the Roman Catholic ecclesiastics of 1560 gave their vote for the Reformation which they so little understood; and where parish law is now different from what it was then, the history of the divergence is not difficult to trace.

---

[1] 'Parish priests are bound—at least *jure ecclesiastico*, and that *sub gravi*—to reside in their parishes. . . . The duty of residence, which is particularly urgent during contagious diseases, comprises not only the obligation of physical dwelling in the parish, but also,' etc.—*Elements of* [Roman Catholic] *Ecclesiastical Law*, by S. B. Smith, D.D., 1887, i. pp. 438-9.

www.ingramcontent.com/pod-product-compliance
Lightning Source LLC
Chambersburg PA
CBHW031401160426
43196CB00007B/848